The Home Concepts Book

First Edition

The Home
Concepts
contemporary designs for modern homes
Book

First Edition

Essential Inspiration for anyone planning,
constructing or just dreaming of a self build

Paul Molloy
With
Visuals by PixelBrick

Shoreline Press

Published by Shoreline Press,
First Floor,
3 Strand St Great,
Dublin 1,
Ireland

Tel: 00353 1 642 59 79
Fax: 00353 1 642 59 79

First published in 2005

ISBN 0-9550145-0-6

Printed and Bound by:
Standard Printers
Ballybrit Ind Est
Ballybrit
Galway
Ireland

Contents

Introduction

The designs and texts in this book have been assembled as a collection of ideas and concepts to assist you during the various stages of creating your own, one off home, whether you are lying in bed simply dreaming a possibility that may be several years from reality or at a point of digging the foundations there are plenty of ideas that will of assistance and inspiration to you throughout the process.

Design and building a house can be a straight forward process with little or no input from you on design, layout and construction, as you can simply buy a site with full planning permission, contract a builder and some time later you have a housethat is your new home. But since you are seeking to build and live in a one off house, why not have a house designed to suit your precise needs, dreams and desires, as a part of the overall build cost from start to finish, it is a well worth investment.

A home is a sum greater than its parts, a well thought out house can be something special and unique that suits your living requirements but also says something about you and your family. The information within this book and of those recommended at the back, will help you dream up your ideal home and how to develop these ideas into something tangible for an Architect to work from.

User guide and notes

The designs are intended to inspire your ideas for what your house could be, taking parts of one house and mixing with another to create a new, unique design that satisfies your requirements and desires, but if you desire one of the houses as they are shown, please contact the architect of that section and they will be happy to discuss the details with you. Contact details are at the start of their section.

The designs in this book have been built on a 1 square acre site and presented with very little greenery between the house and camera, this has been done to show the design as clearly as possible and to show the ehole hose during the animations. These bare sites stand in contrast to the recommendation of integrating a house into its surrounding landscape through the use of plants, shrubs, bushes and trees.

CD-ROM

The CD is designed to play on a PC running Microsoft Windows 98/NT/2000/XP, if your computer is running a different system; the animations for each house are on the CD as individual QuickTime files which can be found in the movies folder. and played directly through QuickTime.

If you do not have the QuickTime player on your computer, you can install it by following these steps;

- Insert CD
- Open the QuickTime folder
- Double click the installer file
- Follow the instructions
- Once complete you can start viewing the animations with out restarting your computer.

The QuickTime installer file has been downloaded directly from the QuickTime website and checked for viruses. If you would prefer to download it yourself or read up on the software, please visit www.quicktime.com

2. House Design

Introduction

There is much debate over the question of upholding traditional house design or to give licence to alternate styles. This question is asked and debated on a regular basis in the media with no clear outcomes or guidelines. Consider how many towns across the country have had new streets, small shopping centres, hotels, pubs, restaurants, nightclubs added or even just upgraded to cater for the increase in population, the desire for better quality, the demand for greater diversity and choice. There is no question that

Rural Village with modern architecture

this change and development is needed but how it is done is sometimes questionable; have some towns lost their charm and charisma, while others have gained a much needed heartbeat and improved character? In our drive for social and economic development are we sacrificing our cultural landscape or evolving it?

With regard to developing your home, there is also a variety of views on how to maintain our cultural heritage while allowing development to happen in relation to one off housing. Cities and large towns often have an incongruous appearance to them, as can be seen through out the country in new office buildings, industrial

Efficiencies (see chapter 5 pg 157). Designing your home to fulfill these recommendations will greatly influence the shape, style, size and positioning of your home.

The designs in this book range from traditional bungalows, dormers and two storey houses to modern adaptations of these to other very contemporary house designs. As the books title describes these designs are concepts, intended to give ideas and inspire your thoughts to what your home could be. Regardless of the design you eventually submit for planning, what will enable your home to integrate with its surroundings is developing the right design for the site and local environment. You can

Top: The dropped in look
Below: An integratred house

Contemporary Irish Architecture

parks, hotels and so forth which have a variety of contemporary and traditional styles. These differences can be seen quite clearly as you drive around the country, and this variation can effect the style and size of house you will arrive at depending on the environment and surrounds that you will finish up with.

Another area that will affect the design of your home is Environmental Impact & Energy

also avoid the drop-in look by planning your site's landscape during the initial design stage, this area is covered in greater detail in section 4

Requirements

Ask yourself, What is your house for? Obvious enough question. 'It's to be our home, where we will live, eat and sleep, raise our kids, invite our friends ' Take a moment to write down as many answers as you can think of to this very pertinent question, try to use words of expression 'happy, warm, fresh ' or phrases 'easy to clean, easy to heat ' or functions 'ability to have dinner parties and not wake the kids, easy access to adequate storage '. The list can be endless and of great detail, however by listing out all you want from your house is a worthwhile exercise and will greater ensure that you end up at the result you desire.

With your list of requirements it is now worth rating each point in order of importance, 5 being high down the scale to 1 being low. It is possible for a well designed house to do all that you dream of but what are the most important aspects that should be known before designing? knowing what your priorities are will bring you in the right direction of designing and achieving your ideal home.

By having a clear list of what is important (and being aware of what is less important) it becomes very easy to identify themes, ideas, images and examples of what you have in mind. This leads to the next step of creating your mood/style board.

The Mood/Style Board

A mood/style board should inspire you and give visual representation to the concepts forming in your mind. It can be a large board or scrap book with lots of pictures taken from magazines, photographs, books, the internet, in fact any source that inspires you! Then interlace your ideas board with descriptive words and phrases taken from the list described above. With your prioritised list and mood/style board it will be much simpler to communicate your requirements for your ideal home to an architect. The more any

architect knows about their client's requirements, the better they are positioned to create a successful design.

From this point on, you and the architect can develop an ideal, build-able and durable home to suit your requirements, budget and dreams.

Mood/Style Board

It would be advisable to read the section on Environmental Impact & Energy Efficiencies, followed by the recommended resources before getting stuck into the initial design stage. This will enable you to integrate these technologies and concepts into your house from the very start, as trying to amend a design later can be difficult, time consuming and costly.

Form Follows Function

The interior layouts of the designs in this book have been shown as 3 Dimensional floor plans to give a greater idea of their spatial layout. Often houses are designed from the outside in, with insufficient thought given to the practicality and usefulness of the interior layout.

Spend time considering what rooms you require, how these rooms may be utilized, with what frequency and what is their end-use? Working through these questions, will allow you to design a house which will first and foremost cover these internal requirements and secondly will start to give shape to the exterior. Future planning should also be considered, what happens as the family expands or in the long-term reduces as children grow and eventually move out. Can your design be easily extended or reduced? Can rooms be converted to other uses with ease? Are you maximizing the potential of your home, for now and the future.

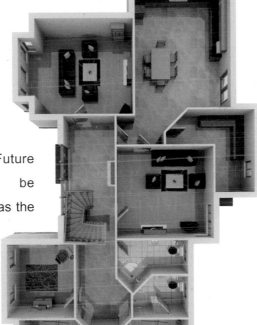

3D Floor Plan

Again making a list of the rooms you require will really help. Start with the primary areas first eg the kitchen, master bedroom, sitting room. Work your way through all areas of the house, considering how each of these rooms/areas are to be used, when they are to be used and how often they are to be used.

Consider the following:

- Should the main communal area be an open plan kitchen - dining room - sitting room so the
- family can be together while doing various activities?
- Do you want a separate dining room or sitting room for special occasions?
- Bathrooms, en suites, WCs how many and for who?
- Is a play room that can later become a study worthwhile?
- Do you need an entrance porch for coats and shoes.
- Is a utility room for laundry, cleaning items and mucky boots practical?
- How much storage space will you require? This can be viewed in time spans of short, medium and long term. Size and location of storage space for these requirements can vary greatly and is worth considering before detailing a design.

Kitchen & Dining

The kitchen is widely considered the heart of the home and can be a great place to start designing from. Many kitchens are combination cooking, dining and living areas, making this area the epicentre of the house

Whilst the positives to this layout are apparent, there are some draw backs such as smells from the kitchen being omnipresent and after dinner the kitchen is still visible which can be a distraction from relaxing, particularly for those that did the cooking!

A separate or second dining area for special occasions is a multifarious choice. In many homes it is a totally separate room, only used once a month, the rest of the time collecting dust but in other layouts it connects to the kitchen and/or sitting room via double or French doors allowing this separate dining area to be more multi-functional in a social setting.

Home office/Study

Play, TV, Games and Study rooms

These room end-uses can be created in one room and only defined by who is using it and for what means. A lot of this breaks down on your requirements, space availability and/or stage in life.

Family Bathroom

Bedrooms & Bathrooms

The bedroom is a sanctuary for personal space, where one can find peace and quite, privacy and solace from a busy house or even a calm one for that matter. A bedroom is a place where one goes to sleep, rest, read, be intimate, recover or be alone. An adult's bedroom can be a very private place that others seldom see but for children and teenagers it's space to bring their friends into, to hang out and do their own thing. All this should be reflective in the bedroom layout of your home.

How many bathrooms? An en suite for all bedrooms has its pros and cons, it will certainly eliminate queues in the morning and give privacy but can also reduce interaction of the household and transparency for parents

Hallways, Landings and Staircases

"But a hall is more than just an entrance; it is a very useful room. Often it encloses the stairs and helps to insulate other rooms from the noise of traffic between floors. It is a neutral space into which you can invite strangers. It provides a transition between outdoors and indoors." Quote by Unkown

Returned staircase with Balcony

As the staircase is the first large feature seen on entering most houses its style will greatly influence the rest of the house leading from it. Before designing a staircase it is best refering to the building regulations as there are certain criteria that must be met.

Staircases can be designed beyond function and into a centre piece achieved through size, shape and constructed materials. A light framed staircase can assist the impression of space which may be desired for a minimalist look, alternatively a heavy set style may add grandeur for a more classical appearance.

Front and Back porches

The front porch is where you will welcome people into your home, possibly hang coats, leave umbrellas or other wet clothing etc.

A back porch is more often combined with being a utility room for laundry and storage, while still maintaining the function of being a place to take off mucky boots, keep pet foods and other paraphernalia that may be odorous or unsightly.

Other very important aspects and efficient benefits of having these areas is to
- create a thermal buffer;
- Minimises drafts
- Stops cold air flowing into the house as soon as a front or back door is opened.
- Keeps the moisture from wet attire isolated.

Storage

Adequate storage is a must for any house. It provides places to keep seasonal items for winter and/or summer, important tools and appliances that are seldom used but no matter how much storage you have, it does have a tendency to get filled.

Well planned and designed storage space will hold what you need but be unsuitable for items that should really be disposed off, recycled or given to charity.

Planning Applications

This is an area that applies general national standards with just minimal details differing from council to council. However it is strongly recommended that before you start designing your home you contact your County Council and get a copy of their planning application forms and guidelines. See pages 169-170

Your architect or engineer will have experience in this area and should advise you on the process and how best to approach it. The ease of attaining planning permission will greatly depend on the location, size, design and integration into the surrounding environment of your proposed development.

Nearly any design of house has the ability to get planning approval, once the design is suitable to the location and presented correctly in plan and reality. Driving from county to county, urban to

rural, you will notice a vast array of house types, styles and sizes, exposed & hidden. Some of these houses would not even be considered for planning in certain counties and areas, while some could attain planning nearly anywhere in the country. This variation in what is realistically achievable should be considered when approaching your design.

Contemporary home - *Pg 127*

In building your own home it is important to consider some other priorities of importance;
Location (close to family & friends, schools & shops, main roads)?
Geography and surroundings (beside the sea, amidst rolling hills, surrounded by woodlands)?
Style and design (exciting, grand or abstract shape of house)?
Cost of land (Affordable plot in a great location or an expansive one in a remote location)?

Giving time to consider all of the above could prevent problems later on when trying to get planning for a style of house in the wrong location. For example, if you want your home overlooking a lake in an area of renowned beauty, a contemporary looking house that stands out from its site will not work with the planners. Alternatively a house design that is consistent with the area, well blended into its environment will have a greater chance of success. If on the other hand, a contemporary looking house was your priority, you may want to consider a different location that will potentially add more value to your ability to attain planning.

Further information is attainable through your County Council and some of the recommended reference material at the back of this book.

Future Proofing

What is future proofing? It is the ability of your home to stand the test of time both aesthetically

The material finish of a house can dramatically change its appearance and the level of maintenance required.

and practically. It is the area that affects various parts of your home at various stages of its life.

Look first at the weathering of your home through the choice of materials it is built from. There are many materials that can look impressive and seem cost effective but will dilapidate rapidly and require maintenance or replacement to keep in functioning order. It is extremely worthwhile to research and really consider what materials you

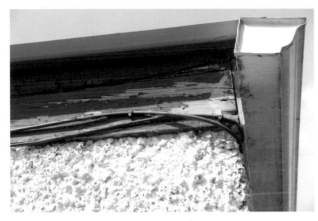

dilapidated roof materials

plan to use. For example choosing a painted render finish for your exterior will require painting every couple of years, aluminium or PVC facia boards will last longer and not require regular painting. Alternatively being able to paint your

walls and facia gives you the option to change the colour and appearance of your house, which is something not feasible with a stone or brick finish.

Placing more than required power sockets, phone and TV points around the house can give good options in the future if you decide to change the layout of a room or convert it to suit a different purpose, perhaps turning a play room into an office/study room. Many have encountered frustration that their TV can only be located in one area of the room due to the arrangement of power and cable points.

Depending on your situation now, your home may require more bedrooms in a few years time as your family expands or less as kids become adults and move out making many rooms redundant. Planning ahead can make the conversion of bedrooms into walk-in wardrobes, a study or hobby room much easier. Perhaps the conversion of two rooms into a self contained flat for an elderly relative or the possibility of just living in the downstairs portion of the house if mobility in old age or illness demands so.

Other areas to consider are the arrangement of rooms that can be extended with sun rooms or conservatories, sliding doors to connect a room to the garden.

There are many things worth considering when it comes to the future of your home, to what detail you care to plan is up to you, but it is highly recommended that you do, to some extent.

David Quinn

Mexlib Design
and Management

Sheeaun Park, Athenry, Co. Galway

P: 091 850 532 . F: 091 850 532 . E: dq@iol.ie

Front Persepctive View

Dimensions

Kitchen	16.6m^2 / 179ft^2
Dining	11.4m^2 / 123ft^2
Sitting	14m^2 / 151ft^2
Living	11.5m^2 / 124ft^2

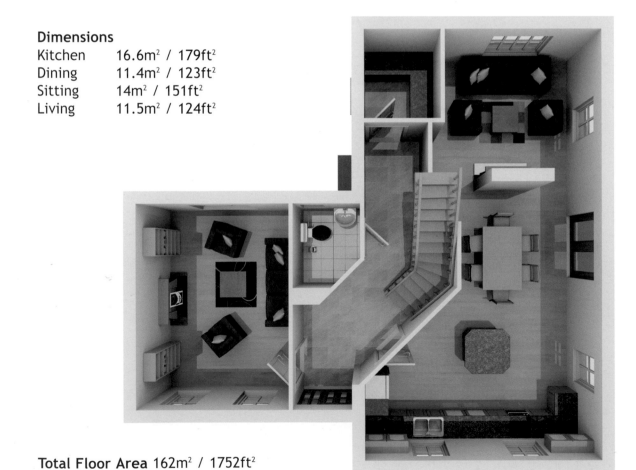

Total Floor Area 162m^2 / 1752ft^2

Ground Floor Plan

Dimensions
Bedroom 1 17.7m² / 191ft²
Bedroom 2 12.2m² / 132ft²
Bedroom 3 10.8m² / 1171ft²

Basic Footprint
Width   11.6m² / 38ft²
Depth   9.6m² / 32ft²
Area   111m² / 1199ft²

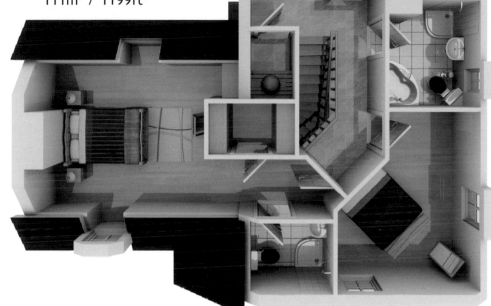

First Floor Plan

Rear Perspective View

Front Persepctive View

Basic Footprint

Width	20.1m² / 66ft²
Depth	16.3m² / 54ft²
Area	327m² / 3532ft²

Dimensions

Kitchen	36m² / 389ft²
Dining	23.3m² / 252ft²
Sitting	20.7m² / 224ft²
Living	28.8m² / 311ft²

Total Floor Area 307m² / 3316ft²

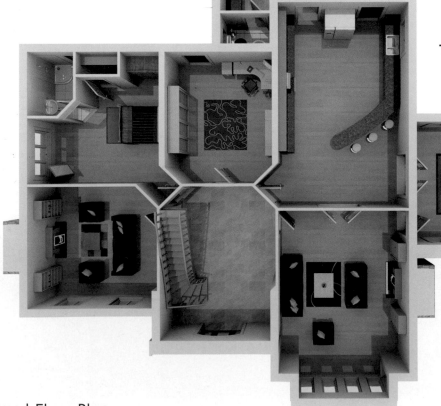

Ground Floor Plan

Dimensions
Bedroom 1 24m² / 259ft²
Bedroom 2 19.3m² / 208ft²
Bedroom 3 16.3m² / 176ft²
Bedroom 4 15.6m² / 168ft²
Bedroom 5 23.4m² / 253ft²

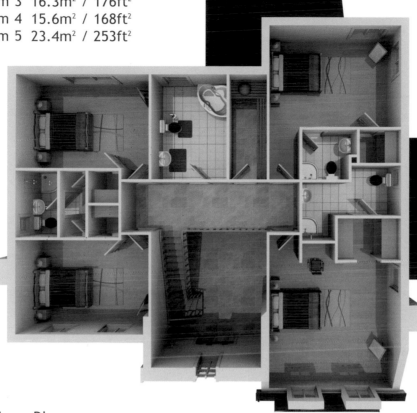

First Floor Plan

Rear Perspective View

Front Persepctive View

Total Floor Area = 10m - 100ft

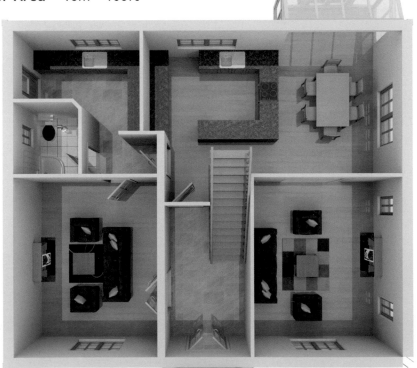

Basic Footprint

Width	11.6m² / 38ft²
Depth	9.8m² / 32ft²
Area	114m² / 1231ft²

Dimensions

Kitchen	18.3m² / 198ft²
Dining	18.2m² / 197ft²
Sitting	20.8m² / 225ft²
Living	21.4m² / 231ft²

Ground Floor Plan

Dimensions
Bedroom 1 17.8m² / 192ft²
Bedroom 2 15.1m² / 163ft²
Bedroom 3 12.8m² / 138ft²

First Floor Plan

Rear Perspective View

Front Persepctive View

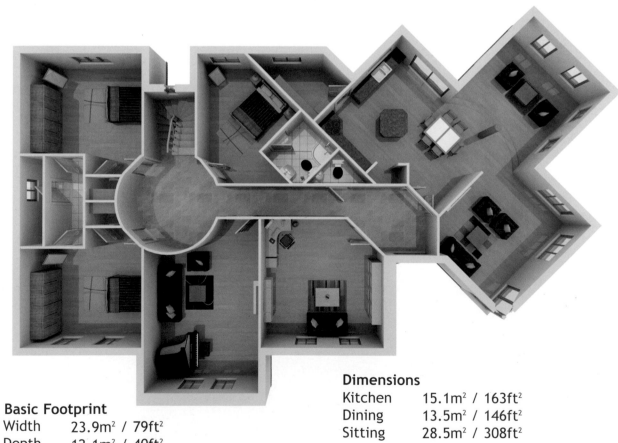

Basic Footprint
Width   23.9m² / 79ft²
Depth   12.1m² / 40ft²
Area   289m² / 3121ft²

Dimensions
Kitchen   15.1m² / 163ft²
Dining   13.5m² / 146ft²
Sitting   28.5m² / 308ft²
Living   19.8m² / 214ft²

Ground Floor Plan

Dimensions
Bedroom 1 31.3m² / 338ft²
Bedroom 2 18.7m² / 202ft²
Bedroom 3 18.7m² / 202ft²
Bedroom 4 15.6m² / 168ft²
Bedroom 5 17.3m² / 187ft²

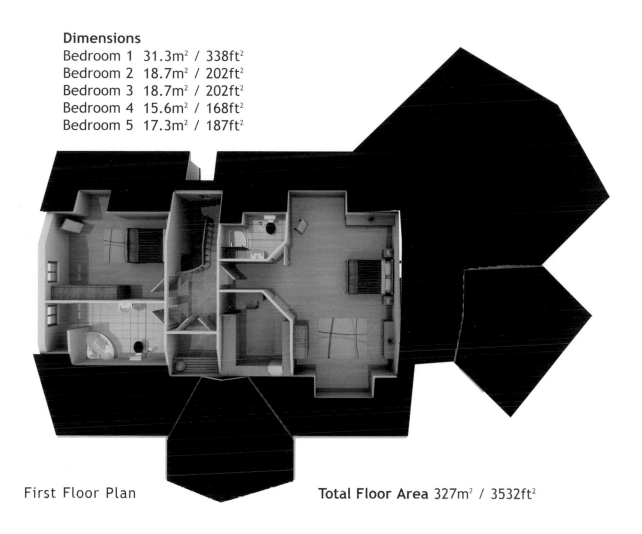

First Floor Plan

Total Floor Area 327m² / 3532ft²

Rear Perspective View

Front Persepctive View

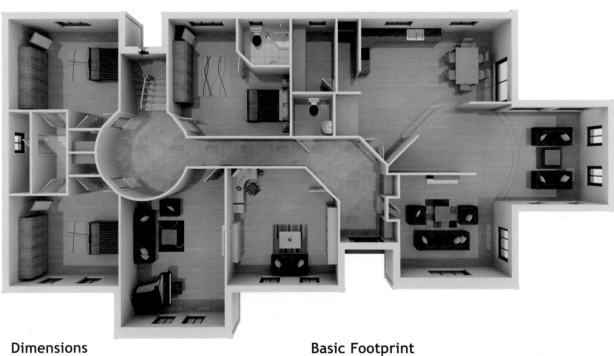

Dimensions

Kitchen	16.4m² / 177ft²
Dining	16.4m² / 177ft²
Sitting	28.5m² / 308ft²
Living	21.2m² / 229ft²

Basic Footprint

Width	26.6m² / 88ft²
Depth	12.1m² / 40ft²
Area	321m² / 3467ft²

Ground Floor Plan

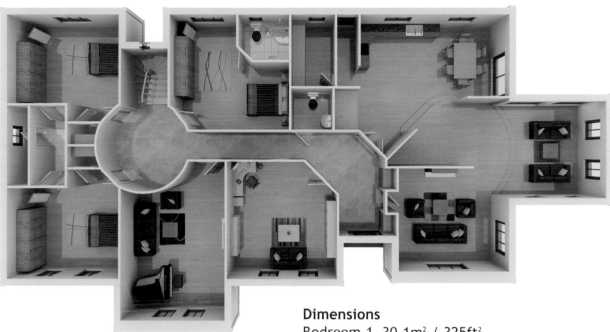

Total Floor Area 352m² / 3802ft²

First Floor Plan

Dimensions
Bedroom 1 30.1m² / 325ft²
Bedroom 2 18.7m² / 202ft²
Bedroom 3 18.7m² / 202ft²
Bedroom 4 15.6m² / 168ft²
Bedroom 5 17.3m² / 187ft²

Rear Perspective View

Front Persepctive View

Total Floor Area 300m² / 3240ft²

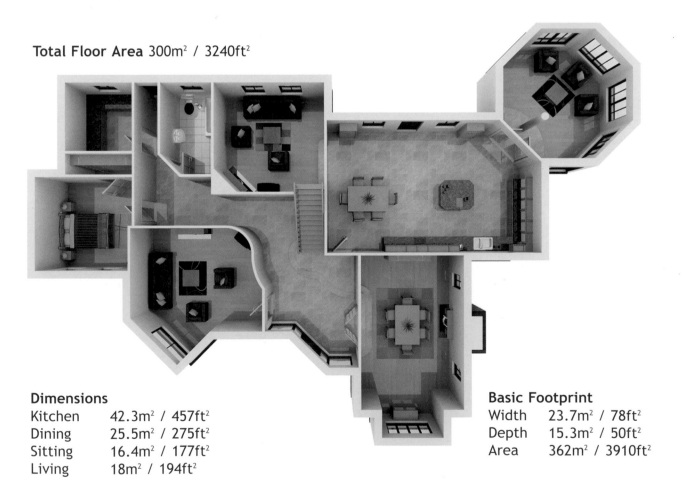

Dimensions
Kitchen 42.3m² / 457ft²
Dining 25.5m² / 275ft²
Sitting 16.4m² / 177ft²
Living 18m² / 194ft²

Basic Footprint
Width 23.7m² / 78ft²
Depth 15.3m² / 50ft²
Area 362m² / 3910ft²

Ground Floor Plan

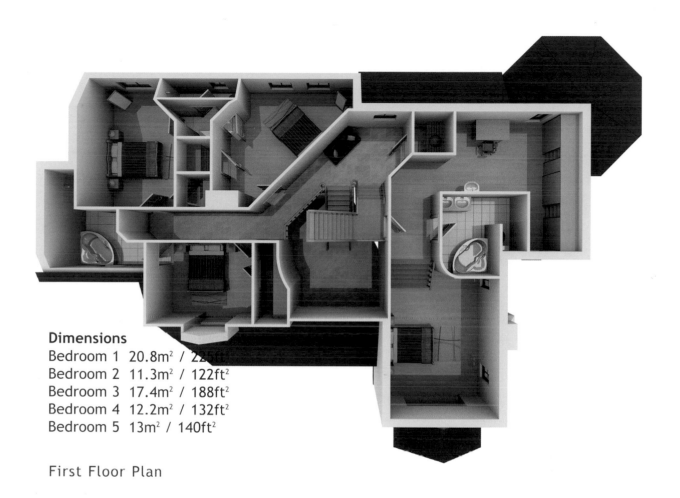

Dimensions
Bedroom 1 20.8m² / 225ft²
Bedroom 2 11.3m² / 122ft²
Bedroom 3 17.4m² / 188ft²
Bedroom 4 12.2m² / 132ft²
Bedroom 5 13m² / 140ft²

First Floor Plan

Rear Perspective View

Front Persepctive View

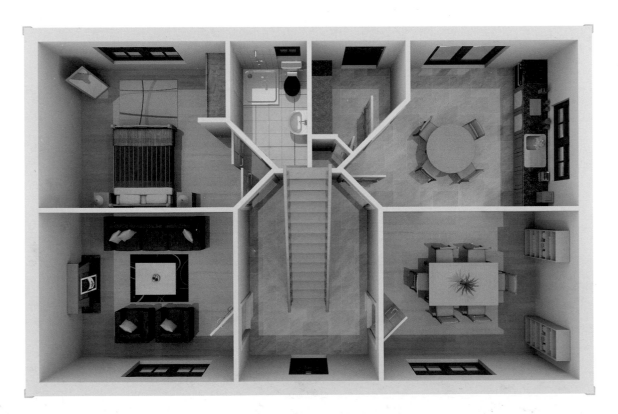

Dimensions
Kitchen   12.6m² / 136ft²
Dining   15.3m² / 165ft²
Sitting   15.3m² / 165ft²

Basic Footprint
Width   12.2m² / 40ft²
Depth   7.9m² / 26ft²
Area   96m² / 1036ft²

Ground Floor Plan

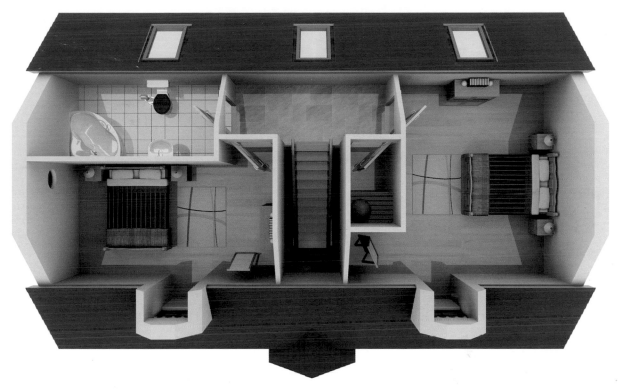

Total Floor Area 139m² / 1501ft²

First Floor Plan

Dimensions
Bedroom 1 14m² / 151ft²
Bedroom 2 18.1m² / 195ft²
Bedroom 3 14.2m² / 153ft²

Rear Perspective View

Front Persepctive View

Dimensions

Kitchen	13.9m^2 / 150ft^2
Dining	13.9m^2 / 150ft^2
Sitting	19.5m^2 / 211ft^2
Bedroom 1	16.5m^2 / 178ft^2
Bedroom 2	17.7m^2 / 191ft^2
Bedroom 3	12m^2 / 130ft^2
Bedroom 4	9.4m^2 / 102ft^2

Basic Footprint

Width	19.6m^2 / 65ft^2
Depth	10m^2 / 33ft^2
Area	196m^2 / 2117ft^2

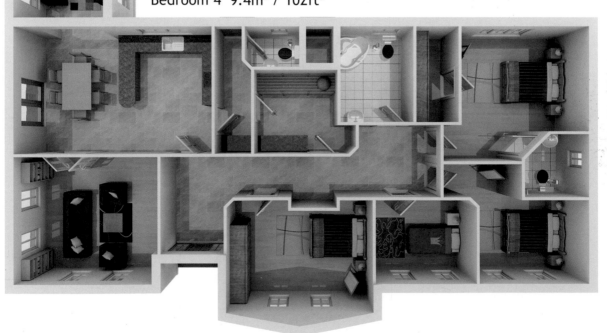

Ground Floor Plan

Total Floor Area 166m^2 / 1793ft^2

Family Bathroom

Rear Perspective View

Front Persepctive View

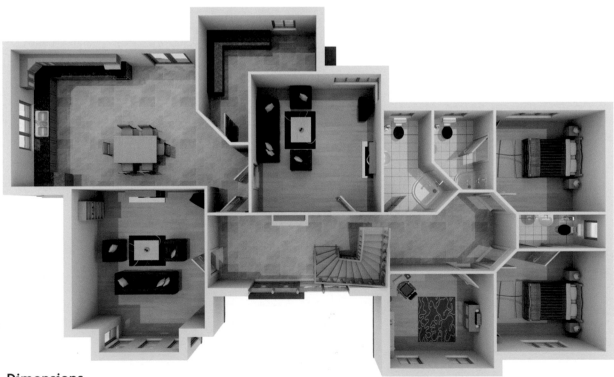

Dimensions

Kitchen   16.1m² / 174ft²
Dining   16.1m² / 174ft²
Sitting   25.5m² / 275ft²
Living   22.8m² / 246ft²

Total Floor Area 290m² / 3132ft²

Ground Floor Plan

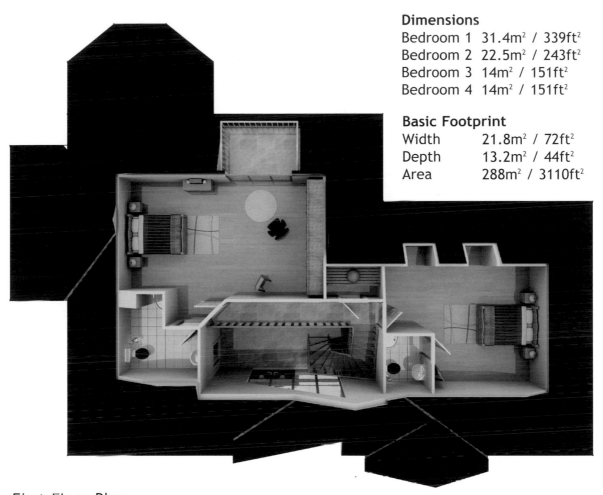

Dimensions
Bedroom 1 31.4m^2 / 339ft^2
Bedroom 2 22.5m^2 / 243ft^2
Bedroom 3 14m^2 / 151ft^2
Bedroom 4 14m^2 / 151ft^2

Basic Footprint
Width   21.8m^2 / 72ft^2
Depth   13.2m^2 / 44ft^2
Area   288m^2 / 3110ft^2

First Floor Plan

Rear Perspective View

Front Persepctive View

Dimensions

Kitchen	22.4m²	/ 242ft²
Dining	16.1m²	/ 174ft²
Sitting	16.1m²	/ 174ft²
Bedroom 1	14.3m²	/ 154ft²
Bedroom 2	14.3m²	/ 154ft²

Basic Footprint

Width	18.4m²	/ 61ft²
Depth	10.1m²	/ 33ft²
Area	186m²	/ 2007ft²

Total Floor Area 248m² / 2678ft²

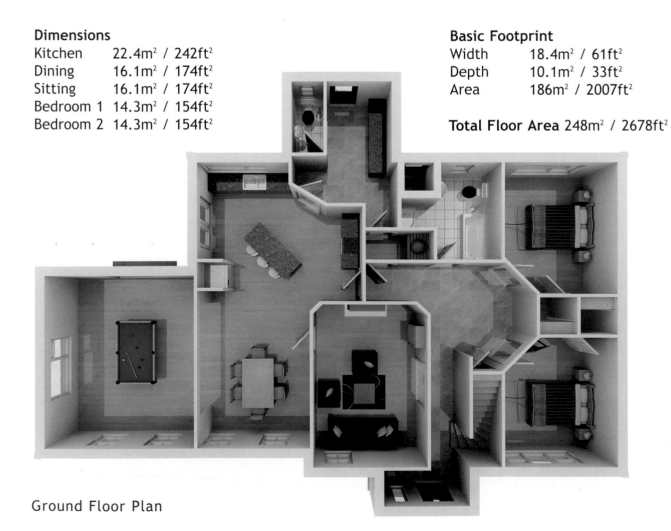

Ground Floor Plan

Sitting Room

Rear Perspective View

Front Persepctive View

Dimensions

Kitchen	15m^2 / 162ft^2
Dining	24.3m^2 / 262ft^2
Sitting	16m^2 / 173ft^2
Living	16.7m^2 / 180ft^2

Basic Footprint

Width	19.9m^2 / 66ft^2
Depth	11.7m^2 / 39ft^2
Area	232m^2 / 2506ft^2

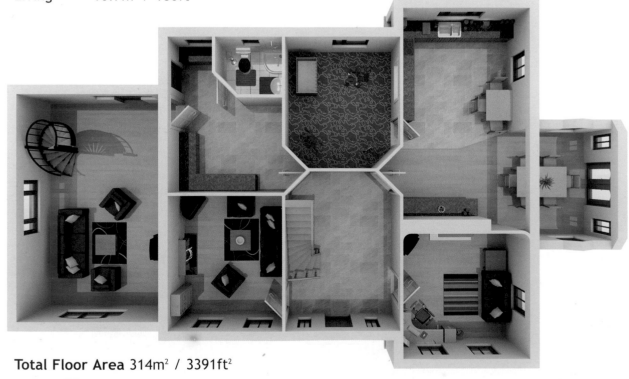

Total Floor Area 314m^2 / 3391ft^2

Ground Floor Plan

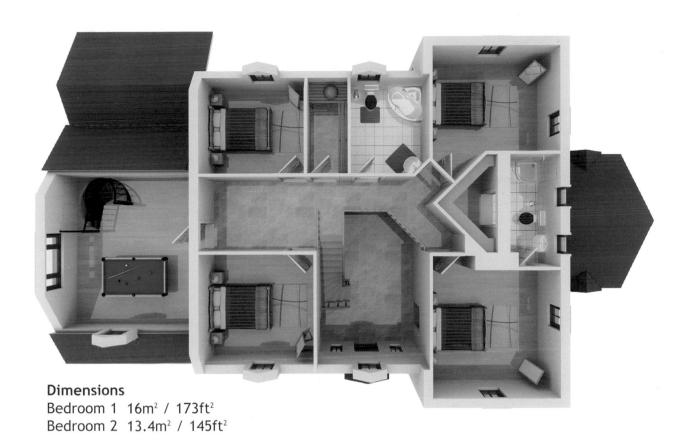

Dimensions
Bedroom 1 16m^2 / 173ft^2
Bedroom 2 13.4m^2 / 145ft^2
Bedroom 3 11.2m^2 / 121ft^2
Bedroom 4 14m^2 / 151ft^2
Bedroom 5 13.4m^2 / 145ft^2

First Floor Plan

Rear Perspective View

Front Persepctive View

Dimensions

Kitchen	15.8m² / 171ft²
Dining	10.5m² / 113ft²
Sitting	18.7m² / 202ft²

Total Floor Area 187m² / 2020ft²

Basic Footprint

Width	12.4m² / 41ft²
Depth	11.9m² / 39ft²
Area	148m² / 1593ft²

Ground Floor Plan

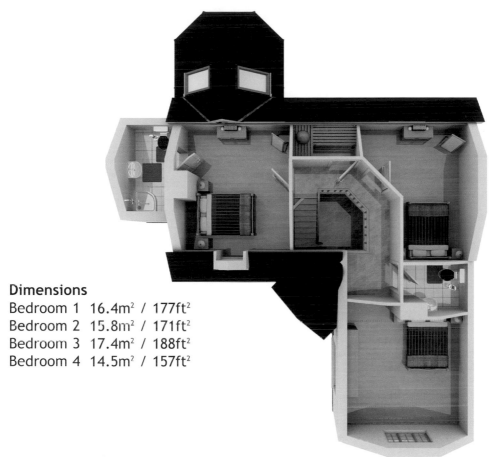

Dimensions
Bedroom 1 16.4m^2 / 177ft^2
Bedroom 2 15.8m^2 / 171ft^2
Bedroom 3 17.4m^2 / 188ft^2
Bedroom 4 14.5m^2 / 157ft^2

First Floor Plan

Rear Perspective View

Front Persepctive View

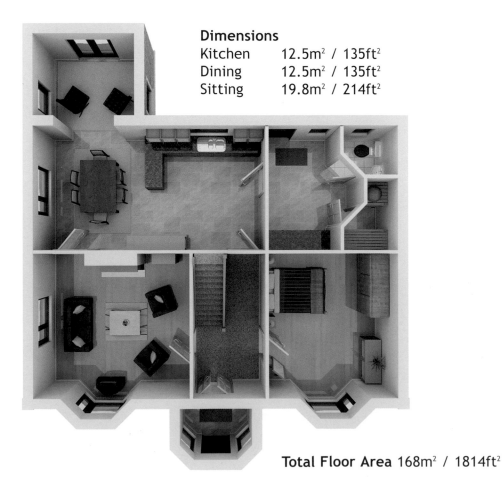

Dimensions
Kitchen   12.5m^2 / 135ft^2
Dining   12.5m^2 / 135ft^2
Sitting   19.8m^2 / 214ft^2

Total Floor Area 168m^2 / 1814ft^2

Ground Floor Plan

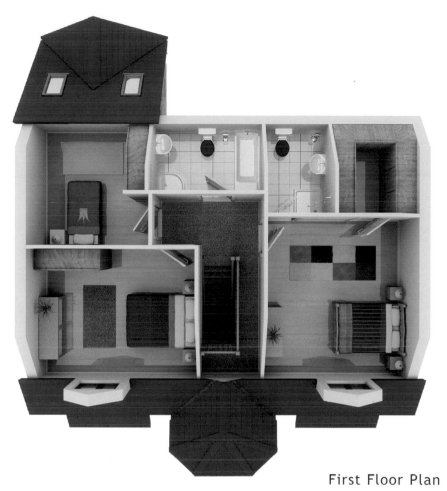

Dimensions
Bedroom 1 16.7m^2 / 180ft^2
Bedroom 2 11.6m^2 / 125ft^2
Bedroom 3 9.3m^2 / 100ft^2
Bedroom 4 16.3m^2 / 176ft^2

Basic Footprint
Width   11.9m^2 / 39ft^2
Depth   8.6m^2 / 28ft^2
Area   102m^2 / 1102ft^2

First Floor Plan

Rear Perspective View

Front Persepctive View

Dimensions
Kitchen 19.8m^2 / 214ft^2
Sitting 19.3m^2 / 208ft^2
Dining 17.5m^2 / 189ft^2

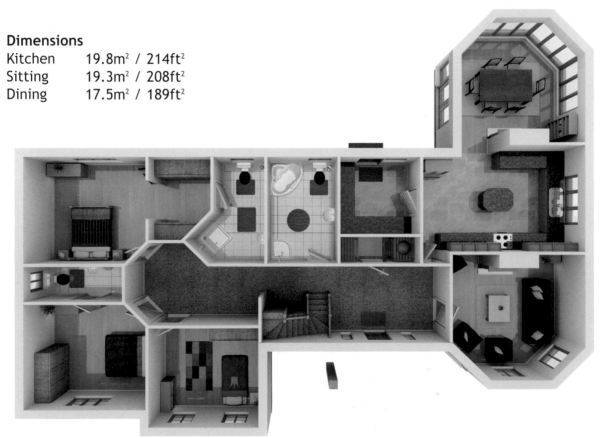

Total Floor Area 218m^2 / 2354ft^2

Ground Floor Plan

Dimensions
Bedroom 1 15m² / 162ft²
Bedroom 2 15m² / 162ft²
Bedroom 3 12.6m² / 136ft²
Bedroom 4 56.6m² / 611ft²

Basic Footprint
Width 19.7m² / 65ft²
Depth 9.2m² / 30ft²
Area 181m² / 1955ft²

First Floor Plan

Rear Perspective View

Front Persepctive View

Dimensions

Kitchen	15.7m² / 170ft²
Dining	35m² / 378ft²
Sitting	21.5m² / 232ft²
Living	33m² / 356ft²
Bedroom 1	41m² / 443ft²
Bedroom 2	13.2m² / 143ft²
Bedroom 3	18.7m² / 202ft²
Bedroom 4	13.6m² / 147ft²
Bedroom 5	15.3m² / 165ft²

Total Floor Area 412m² / 4450ft²

Basic Footprint

Width	20m² / 66ft²
Depth	14.6m² / 48ft²
Area	292m² / 3154ft²

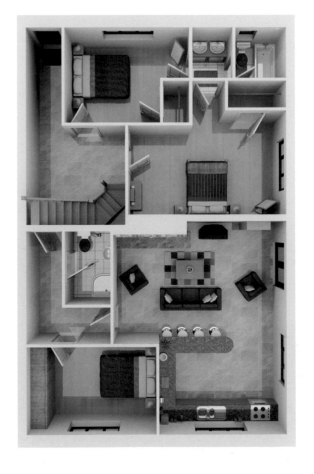

Basement

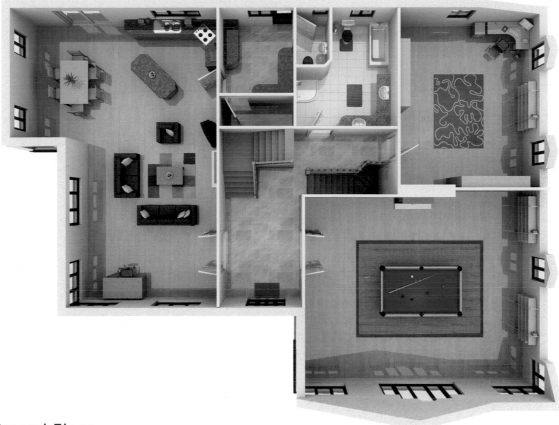

Ground Floor

Rear Perspective View

Front Persepctive View

Dimensions

Kitchen	20.5m² / 221ft²
Dining	15.6m² / 168ft²
Sitting	28.8m² / 311ft²
Living	24.7m² / 267ft²
Utility	

Kitchen   20.5m^2 / 221ft^2
Dining   15.6m^2 / 168ft^2
Sitting   28.8m^2 / 311ft^2
Living   24.7m^2 / 267ft^2
Utility

Total Floor Area 440m^2 / 4752ft^2

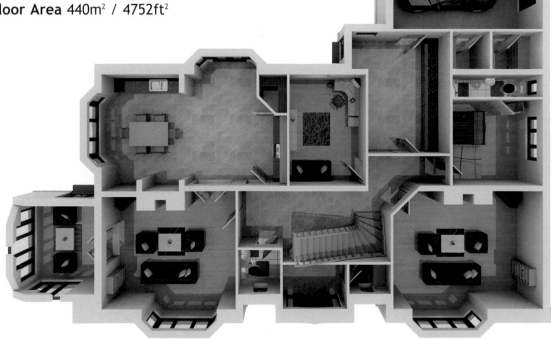

Ground Floor Plan

Dimensions

Bedroom 1 27m^2 / 292ft^2
Bedroom 2 19.2m^2 / 207ft^2
Bedroom 3 21.2m^2 / 229ft^2
Bedroom 4 19.6m^2 / 212ft^2
Bedroom 5 21.3m^2 / 230ft^2

Basic Footprint

Width   22.3m^2 / 74ft^2
Depth   16.6m^2 / 55ft^2
Area   370m^2 / 3996ft^2

First Floor Plan

Rear Perspective View

Front Persepctive View

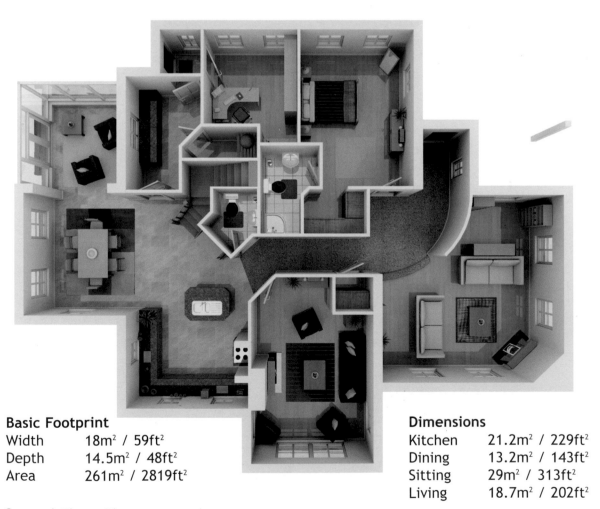

Basic Footprint

Width	18m² / 59ft²
Depth	14.5m² / 48ft²
Area	261m² / 2819ft²

Dimensions

Kitchen	21.2m² / 229ft²
Dining	13.2m² / 143ft²
Sitting	29m² / 313ft²
Living	18.7m² / 202ft²

Ground Floor Plan

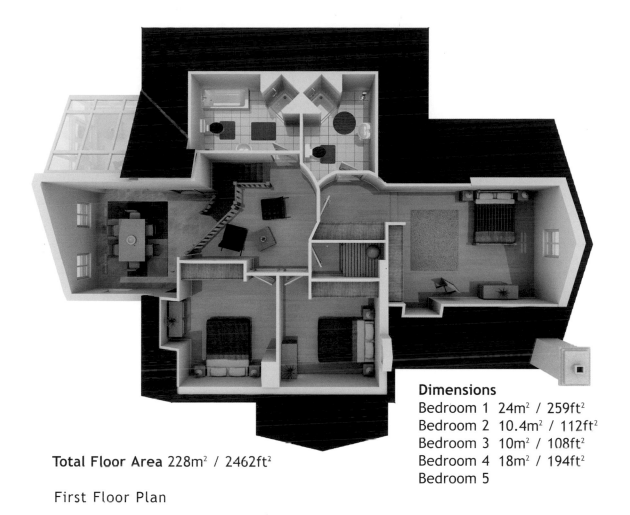

Total Floor Area 228m² / 2462ft²

First Floor Plan

Dimensions
Bedroom 1 24m² / 259ft²
Bedroom 2 10.4m² / 112ft²
Bedroom 3 10m² / 108ft²
Bedroom 4 18m² / 194ft²
Bedroom 5

Rear Perspective View

Front Persepctive View

Dimensions

Kitchen 14.5m² / 157ft²
Dining 8.3m² / 90ft²
Living 18.5m² / 200ft²
Bedroom 1 12.2m² / 132ft²
Bedroom 2 10m² / 108ft²
Bedroom 3 10m² / 108ft²

Total Floor Area 140m² / 1512ft²

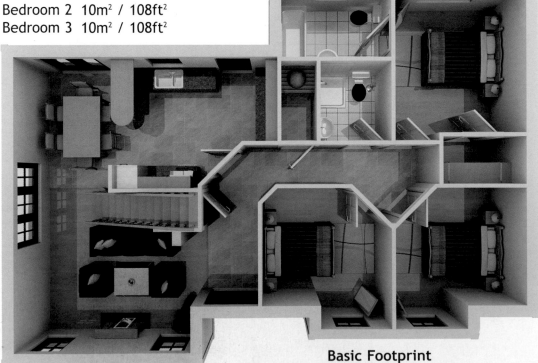

Ground Floor Plan

Basic Footprint

Width 13.7m² / 45ft²
Depth 9.6m² / 32ft²
Area 132m² / 1426ft²

Kitchen/Dining

Rear Perspective View

Front Persepctive View

Dimensions

		Basic Footprint	
Kitchen	16m² / 173ft²	Width	17.2m² / 57ft²
Dining	16m² / 173ft²	Depth	10.2m² / 34ft²
Sitting	37m² / 400ft²	Area	175m² / 1890ft²

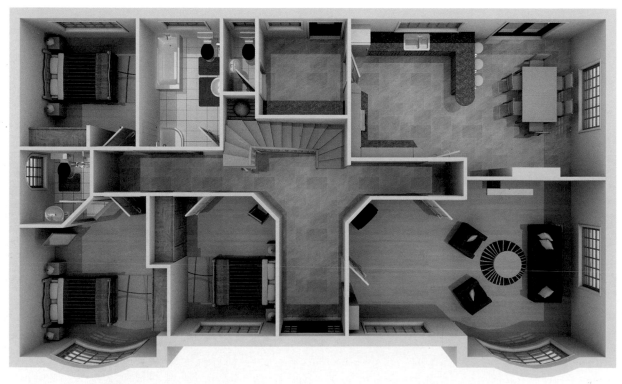

Ground Floor Plan   **Total Floor Area** 234m² / 2527ft²

Kitchen/Dining

Rear Perspective View

Front Persepctive View

Dimensions
Kitchen   30m² / 324ft²
Sitting   20.4m² / 220²

Basic Footprint
Width   18.7m² / 62ft²
Depth   9.5m² / 31ft²
Area   178m² / 1922ft²

Total Floor Area 316m² / 3413ft²

Ground Floor Plan

Dimensions
Bedroom 1 19.4m² / 210ft²
Bedroom 2 13.9m² / 150ft²
Bedroom 3 14.4m² / 156ft²
Bedroom 4 12.7m² / 137ft²
Bedroom 5 17.2m² / 186ft²

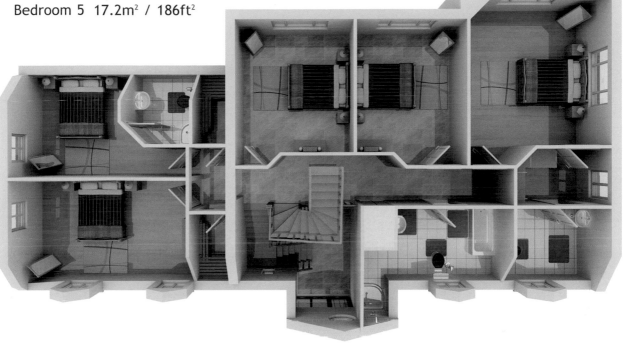

First Floor Plan

Rear Perspective View

Front Persepctive View

Dimensions
Kitchen	12.1m^2 / 131ft^2
Dining	16m^2 / 173ft^2
Sitting	11m^2 / 119ft^2
Living	16.5m^2 / 178ft^2

Total Floor Area 160m^2 / 1728ft^2

Ground Floor Plan

Dimensions
Bedroom 1 27.6m² / 298ft²
Bedroom 2 10.3m² / 111ft²
Bedroom 3 11.5m² / 124ft²

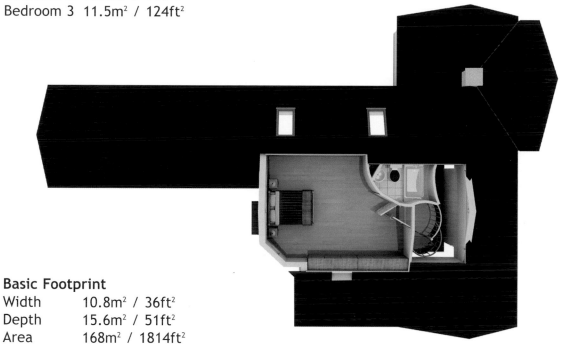

Basic Footprint
Width   10.8m² / 36ft²
Depth   15.6m² / 51ft²
Area   168m² / 1814ft²

First Floor Plan

Rear Perspective View

3. Finding a Site

1. Requirements
2. Assessment & Selection

Requirements

Choosing and buying your site is the first step and commitment to the process of building your own home. The initial considerations are; where do you want to live, the location of the site, what is your budget, is the quality of the site more important than the size?

All these things need to be given some thought.

Some of these questions may seem basic enough, but if left unasked and unanswered, the ramifications over time can be considerable. For example, what if the location is not a comfortable commuting distance to and from your place of work or your childrens school? The journey may seem fine at first but when your travelling this distance every day for some time, it may begin to impede on the quality of life you are endeavouring to establish by buying your own site and building your own home.

The following list may help clarify what your ideal site will be, the clearer the idea you have of the type of site you want and the location it should be in, the easier it will be to find.

Consider the following:
- Distance from shops, schools (or school bus route) and your place of employment.
- Quality of road network in the area
- Existence of other homes which would indicate water, electricity and telecoms linkage to an area.
- Check council plans to see what is planned for the area.
- Size of plot to location in relation to your budget. A quarter acre in a great location could cost the same as one acre in an average location.

Once you have a clear idea of what you want, it is time to investigate what is available. Sites are
- advertised in several ways, such as:
- Newspapers : local and national
  Web sites such as www.myhome.ie,
- www.daft.ie and www.sitefinder.ie

www.sitefinderireland.ie

Estate agents (windows, website, newsletters
- & mailing lists)
  Small signs on back roads

This exercise will bring a variety of results, particularly the latter two as there are a number of estate agents and auctioneers that advertise a

Just a sign for advertising

site by just putting a sign on the side of the road. When you have identified the area in which you would like your site to be located, get an Ordinance Survey map of the area and drive around all the roads looking for any signs. There
- are many benefits to this process:
- Getting to know the area you are interested in. Having already researched sites through conventional means and having this list with you, it will be easy to locate exactly where they are and what the area is like before
- arranging to view in detail.
  You can time how long it takes to get from the different sites to town, place of work, schools, etc.

Assessment and Selection

When you have drawn up a list of potential sites that meet your requirements, it is time to view them. Arrange this with the Estate agent or landowner as they may need or wish to go with you and the landowner will need to know that there will be people on their land. Bear in mind that they can also give you valuable information for taking into consideration.

The following steps are based on information in the HomeBond 'House Building Manual' (see recommended reading pg.171)

Step 1.

Look at existing buildings adjoining your site or in the immediate area for the following;

- Subsidence - usually presents as cracks in the building

Cracks caused by subsidence

- Position or spacing - Are there houses oddly positioned or spaced in relation to adjoining buildings. If so, why? This could be down to underground piping, areas of marshy ground or other.

- Exposure to the elements - is one side of a house noticeably more worn than the others
- How do other properties back onto the site, as most one off houses will have a septic tank and percolation area or reed bed, these can smell, especially in summer. So how does this positioning relate to the site, as percolation areas follow the downward slope away from the house?

Step 2.

Assess the site for its level of exposure to the elements and your level of privacy. Talk to locals to find out about weather conditions throughout the year and from which direction the wind blows (this is useful in relation to smells as noted above), as this will effect the thermal cooling of the building and how you use your garden in summer.

Step 3.

Also research the history of the site:

- Are there a lot of historic ruins in the area?
- Is the site low lying, on a filled in pond or waste area?
- Is it prone to flooding in heavy rain and when local streams swell?
- What is growing on the site? Is the growth associated with ground of high water content or dry sandy soil (the latter will effect your

Sites near or below water table level can be prone to flooding

garden more than the house)?

- Has the site been built on before? If so for what usage?

Step 4.

Access to the site and what is happening in the area are also important points to consider:

- Will you have your own access to the site or will it be shared?

- Can an entrance be positioned on a safe section of the main road? This is also a planning requirement so ensure you check the relevant county's planning guidelines for additional information (Contact details on pg 169).

- Check for other sites for sale, adjoining or in the locality of the one you are interested in for planning applications and the county development plan, all available at the county council offices or website

Before you start viewing, read the relevant County Council's planning guidelines and other material on site selection, as mentioned above. As it is very difficult to make a bad site into a good one!

When it comes to negotiating the price, try to find out the level of interest. A lack of competition is to your benefit but it could also indicate that there is something wrong with the site. Alternatively a lot of interest is to the sellers benefit. Finally try to find out how much comparable sites are selling for in the area. Simply ask other estate agents how much they believe you should have to pay for a site in the area.

Visible & safe access to the site

Dominic Whoriskey

Dominic Whoriskey
& Associates

Main Street, Letterkenny, Co. Donegal
P: 074 91 56996 . E: dominicwhorisky@eircom.net

Front Persepctive View

Dimensions

Kitchen	25.2m² / 272ft²
Sitting	33m² / 356ft²
Lounge	32.5m² / 352ft²
Office	13.65m² /148ft²

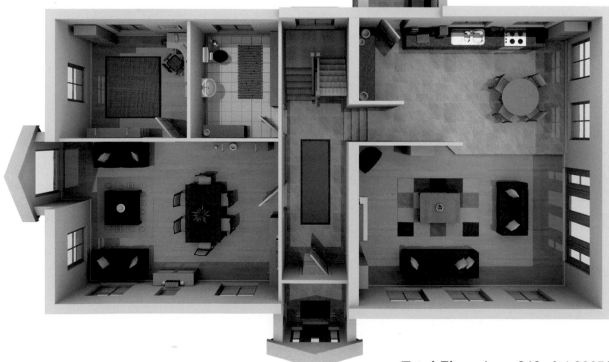

Ground Floor Plan

Total Floor Area 269m² / 2905ft²

Dimensions
Bedroom 1 32.8m² / 354ft²
Bedroom 2 14m² / 151ft²
Bedroom 3 12.25m² / 132ft²
Bedroom 4 10.5m² / 113ft²

Basic Footprint
Width   16.9m² / 56ft²
Depth   11.8m² / 39ft²
Area   200m² / 2160ft²

First Floor Plan

Rear Perspective View

Front Persepctive View

Dimensions

Kitchen	16.8m^2 / 181ft^2
Sitting	22.8m^2 / 246ft^2
Utility	4.4m^2 / 48ft^2

Ground Floor Plan   **Total Floor Area** 242m^2 / 2614ft^2

Dimensions
Bedroom 1 15.8m² / 170ft²
Bedroom 2 22.8m² / 246ft²
Bedroom 3 9.6m² / 104ft²
Bedroom 4 11m² / 119ft²

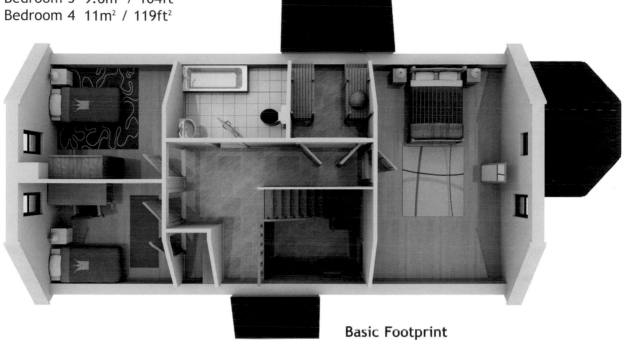

First Floor Plan

Basic Footprint
Width   16.3m² / 54ft²
Depth   7.8m² / 26ft²
Area   127m² / 1373ft²

Rear Perspective View

Front Persepctive View

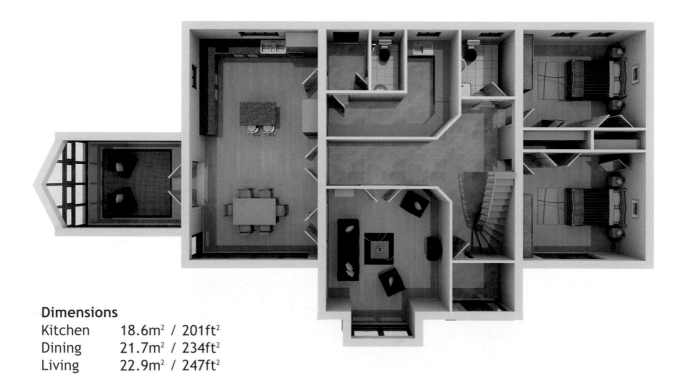

Dimensions

Kitchen   18.6m² / 201ft²
Dining   21.7m² / 234ft²
Living   22.9m² / 247ft²
Utility   11.2m² / 121ft²

Total Floor Area 287m² / 3100ft²

Ground Floor Plan

Basic Footprint
Width   21.9m² / 72ft²
Depth   12m² / 40ft²
Area   263m² / 2838ft²

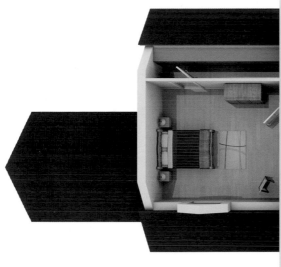
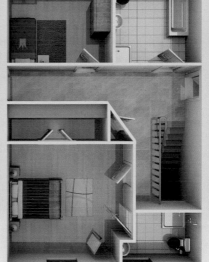

Dimensions
Bedroom 1 15.8m² / 170ft²
Bedroom 2 17.8m² / 192ft²
Bedroom 3 19m² / 205ft²
Bedroom 4 21.6m² / 233ft²
Bedroom 5 11.5m² / 123ft²

First Floor Plan

Rear Perspective View

Front Persepctive View

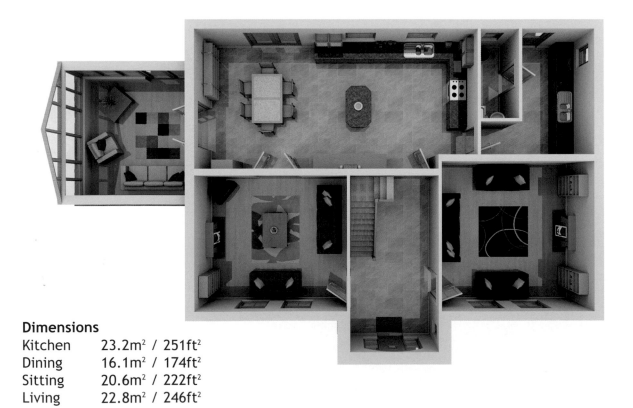

Dimensions

Kitchen	23.2m² / 251ft²	
Dining	16.1m² / 174ft²	
Sitting	20.6m² / 222ft²	
Living	22.8m² / 246ft²	
Utility	8.8m² / 95ft²	

Total Floor Area 249m² / 2689ft²

Ground Floor Plan

Dimensions
Bedroom 1 14.9m^2 / 161ft^2
Bedroom 2 19.2m^2 / 207ft^2
Bedroom 3 16.8m^2 / 181ft^2
Bedroom 4 19.2m^2 / 207ft^2

First Floor Plan

Basic Footprint
Width   17.5m^2 / 58ft^2
Depth   11m^2 / 36ft^2
Area   193m^2 / 2079ft^2

Rear Perspective View

Front Persepctive View

Total Floor Area 284m^2 / 3067ft^2

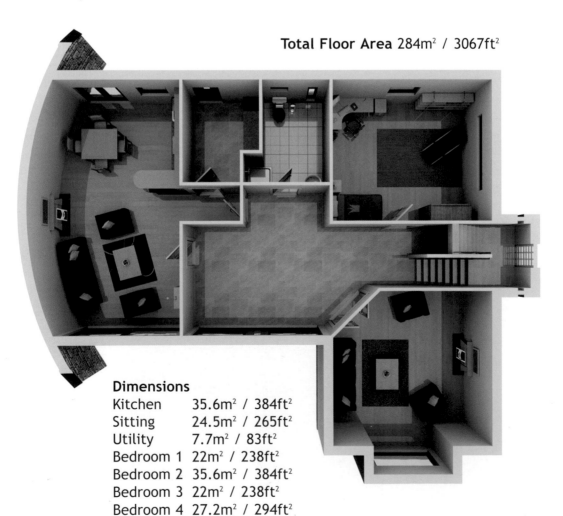

Dimensions

Kitchen 35.6m^2 / 384ft^2
Sitting 24.5m^2 / 265ft^2
Utility 7.7m^2 / 83ft^2
Bedroom 1 22m^2 / 238ft^2
Bedroom 2 35.6m^2 / 384ft^2
Bedroom 3 22m^2 / 238ft^2
Bedroom 4 27.2m^2 / 294ft^2

Ground Floor Plan

First Floor Plan

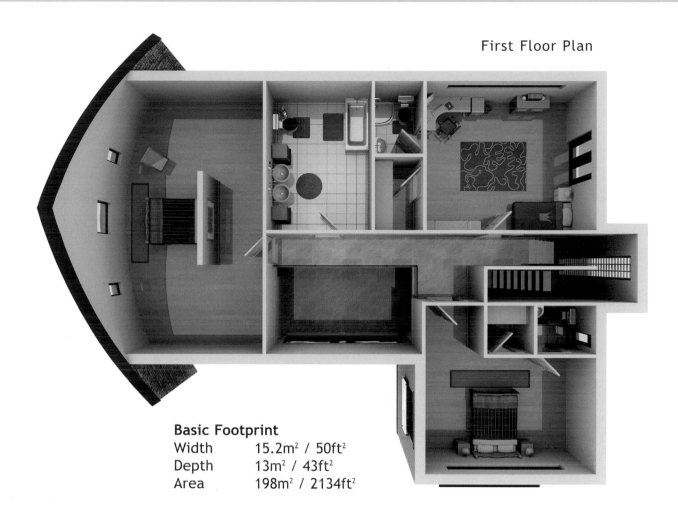

Basic Footprint
Width $15.2m^2$ / $50ft^2$
Depth $13m^2$ / $43ft^2$
Area $198m^2$ / $2134ft^2$

Rear Perspective View

Front Persepctive View

Dimensions

Kitchen	18m²	/ 194ft²
Dining	11.4m²	/ 123ft²
Living	18.45m²	/ 199ft²
Utility	5.2m²	/ 56ft²

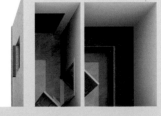

Ground Floor Plan

Total Floor Area 216m² / 2333ft²

Dimensions
Bedroom 1 19.8m² / 214ft²
Bedroom 2 18m² / 194ft²
Bedroom 3 18m² / 194ft²

Basic Footprint

Width	12.75m² / 42ft²
Depth	9.1m² / 30ft²
Area	116m² / 1253ft²

First Floor Plan

Rear Perspective View

Front Persepctive View

Dimensions

Kitchen	25.3m² / 273ft²
Sitting	17.2m² / 186ft²
Utility	4.8m² / 52ft²

Basic Footprint

Width	15.7m² / 52ft²
Depth	8.9m² / 29ft²
Area	140m² / 1509ft²

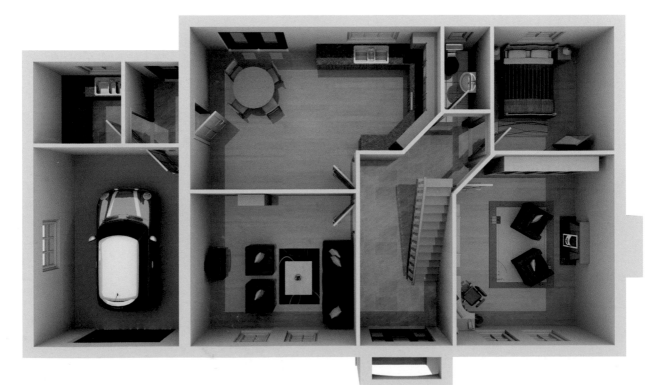

Total Floor Area 200m² / 2160ft²

Ground Floor Plan

Dimensions
Bedroom 1 9.9m² / 107 ft²
Bedroom 2 15.5m² / 167ft²
Bedroom 3 12m² / 130ft²
Bedroom 4 9m² / 97ft²

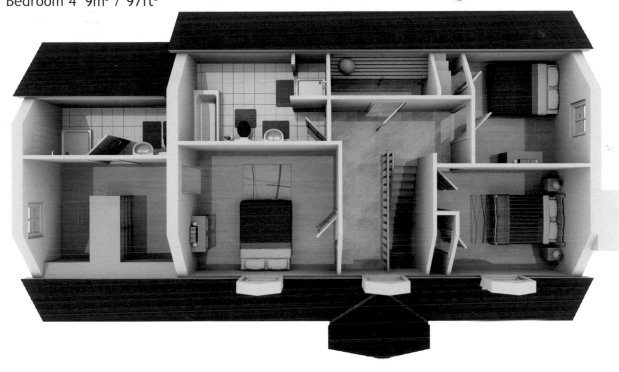

First Floor Plan

Rear Perspective View

Front Persepctive View

Dimensions

Kitchen	26.16m^2 / 283ft^2
Dining	18.8m^2 / 203ft^2
Sitting	20.1m^2 / 217ft^2
Utility	8.7m^2 / 94ft^2

Basic Footprint

Width	22.2m^2 / 73ft^2
Depth	9.9m^2 / 33ft^2
Area	218m^2 / 2350ft^2

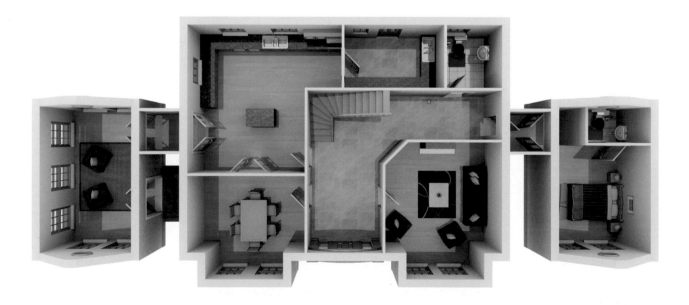

Total Floor Area 240m^2 / 2592ft^2

Ground Floor Plan

Dimensions
Bedroom 1 19.7m^2 / 213ft^2
Bedroom 2 18.8m^2 / 203ft^2
Bedroom 3 17.6m^2 / 190ft^2
Bedroom 4 8.6m^2 / 93ft^2
Bedroom 5 18.4m^2 / 199ft^2

First Floor Plan

Rear Perspective View

Front Persepctive View

Dimensions

Kitchen	25.5m^2	/ 275ft^2
Dining	20.6m^2	/ 222ft^2
Sitting	35m^2	/ 378ft^2
Living	21.1m^2	/ 228ft^2
Utility	9.6m^2	/ 104ft^2

Ground Floor Plan

Total Floor Area 357m^2 / 3856ft^2

Basic Footprint

Width	20.4m² / 67ft²
Depth	10.7m² / 35ft²
Area	218m² / 2354ft²

Dimensions

Bedroom 1	27.1m² / 293ft²
Bedroom 2	15.2m² / 164ft²
Bedroom 3	15.2m² / 164ft²
Bedroom 4	16m² / 173ft²

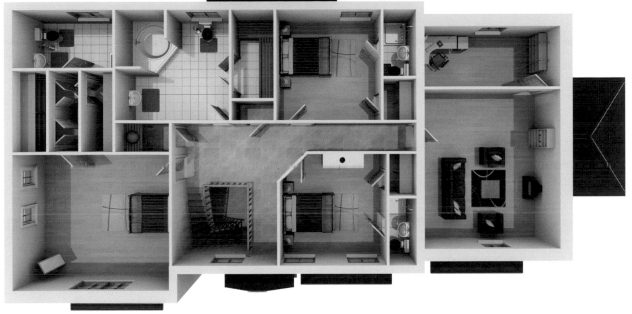

First Floor Plan

Rear Perspective View

Front Persepctive View

Dimensions

Kitchen	16.45m² / 178ft²	
Dining	16.45m² / 178ft²	
Sitting	24.9m² / 269ft²	
Living	9.1m² / 98ft²	
Utility		

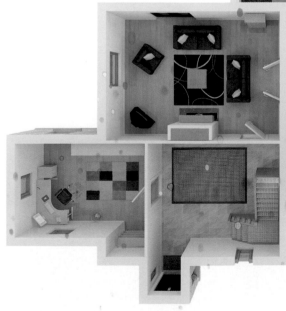

Basic Footprint

Width	18m² / 59ft²
Depth	8.8m² / 29ft²
Area	158m² / 1706ft²

Ground Floor Plan

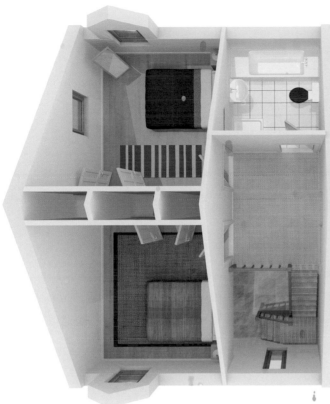

Dimensions
Bedroom 1 23m² / 248ft²
Bedroom 2 12.4m² / 134ft²
Bedroom 3 12.4m² / 134ft²

Total Floor Area 204m² / 2203ft²

First Floor Plan

Rear Perspective View

Front Persepctive View

Dimensions

Kitchen	12.2m^2 / 131.8ft^2	
Dining	13.2m^2 / 142.6ft^2	
Sitting	19.8m^2 / 214ft^2	
Living	17.2m^2 / 186ft^2	
Utility	8.1m^2 / 87ft^2	

Basic Footprint

Width	12.3m^2 / 41ft^2	
Depth	10.4m^2 / 34ft^2	
Area	128m^2 / 1382ft^2	

Total Floor Area 248m^2 / 2678ft^2

Ground Floor Plan

Dimensions
Bedroom 1 $15.8m^2$ / $171ft^2$
Bedroom 2 $13.5m^2$ / $146ft^2$
Bedroom 3 $15.8m^2$ / $171ft^2$
Bedroom 5 $15m^2$ / $162ft^2$

First Floor Plan

Rear Perspective View

Front Persepctive View

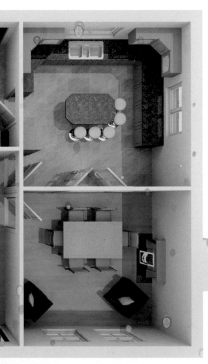

Basic Footprint

Width	11.6m² / 38ft²
Depth	8.9m² / 29ft²
Area	103m² / 1112ft²

Dimensions

Kitchen	18m² / 194ft²
Dining	17.2m² / 186ft²
Sitting	24m² / 259ft²
Utility	8.3m² / 90ft²

Ground Floor Plan

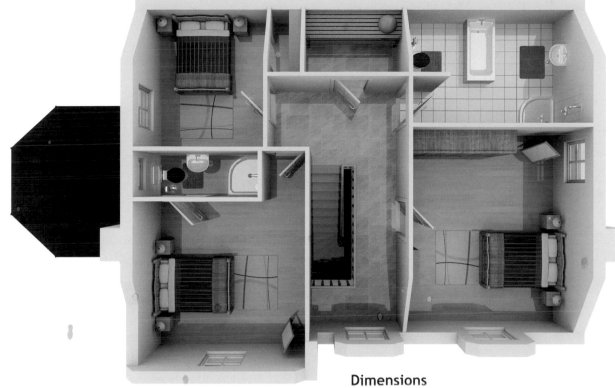

Total Floor Area 205m² / 2214ft²

First Floor Plan

Dimensions
Bedroom 1 21.3m² / 230ft²
Bedroom 2 22m² / 238ft²
Bedroom 3 11.3m² / 122ft²
Bedroom 4 10m² / 108ft²

Rear Perspective View

Front Persepctive View

Dimensions

Kitchen	8.8m^2 / 95ft^2
Dining	18m^2 / 194ft^2
Sitting	10m^2 / 108ft^2
Living	23.8m^2 / 257ft^2
Utility	6.8m^2 / 73ft^2

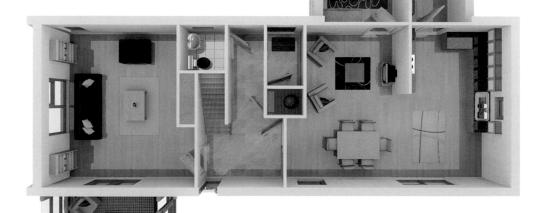

Total Floor Area 178m^2 / 1922ft^2

Ground Floor Plan

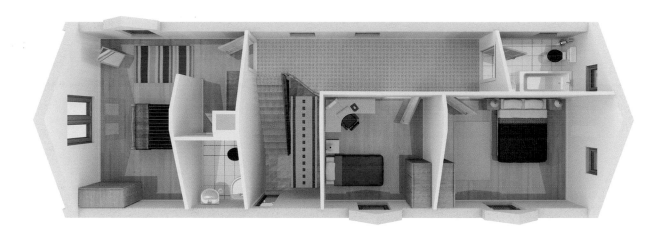

Dimensions
Bedroom 1 19.5m² / 211ft²
Bedroom 2 15.5m² / 167ft²
Bedroom 3 10.9m² / 118ft²
Bedroom 4 9.5m² / 103ft²

Basic Footprint
Width   15.2m² / 50ft²
Depth   9.5m² / 31ft²
Area   144m² / 1555ft²

First Floor Plan

Rear Perspective View

Front Persepctive View

Dimensions

Kitchen	14m² / 151ft²
Living	16m² / 173ft²
Utility	3.6m² / 39ft²

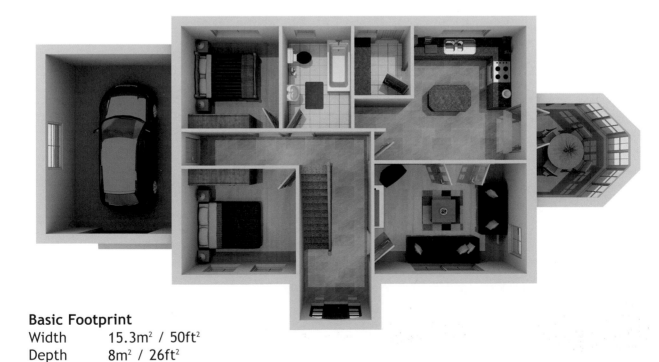

Basic Footprint

Width	15.3m² / 50ft²
Depth	8m² / 26ft²
Area	122m² / 1318ft²

Ground Floor Plan

Dimensions
Bedroom 1 14.1m^2 / 152ft^2
Bedroom 2 11m^2 / 119ft^2
Bedroom 3 9m^2 / 97ft^2

Total Floor Area 194m^2 / 2095ft^2

First Floor Plan

Rear Perspective View

Front Persepctive View

Dimensions

Kitchen	14.4m² / 155ft²
Dining	15m² / 162ft²
Sitting	9.6m² / 104ft²
Living	20.7m² / 224ft²
Utility	7.5m² / 81ft²

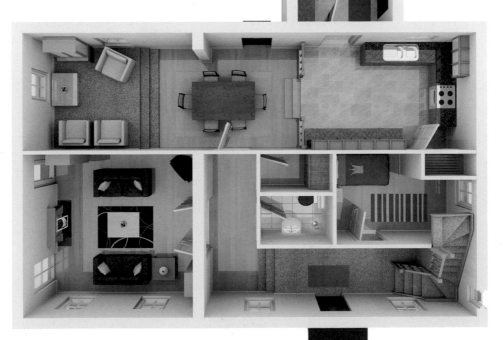

Total Floor Area 202m² / 2182ft²

Ground Floor Plan

Dimensions
Bedroom 1 20.7m² / 224ft²
Bedroom 2 11.5m² / 124ft²
Bedroom 3 11.2m² / 121ft²
Bedroom 4 8.5m² / 92ft²

Basic Footprint
Width   13m² / 43ft²
Depth   8.2m² / 27ft²
Area   107m² / 1151ft²

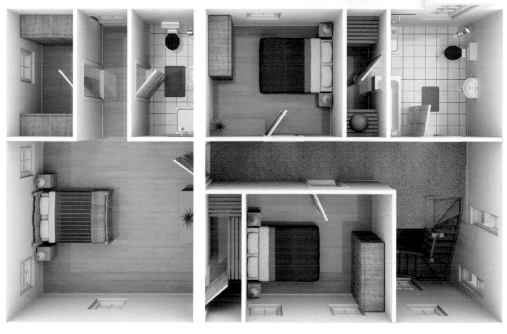

First Floor Plan

Rear Perspective View

Front Persepctive View

Dimensions

Kitchen	17.4m^2 / 188ft^2
Dining	21.9m^2 / 237ft^2
Sitting	29.6m^2 / 320ft^2
Living	23m^2 / 248ft^2
Utility	6.6m^2 / 71ft^2

Basic Footprint

Width	13.6m^2 / 45ft^2
Depth	11.3m^2 / 37ft^2
Area	154m^2 / 1663ft^2

Ground Floor Plan

Dimensions
Bedroom 1 24.2m^2 / 261ft^2
Bedroom 2 16m^2 / 173ft^2
Bedroom 3 19.5m^2 / 211ft^2
Bedroom 4 13.6m^2 / 147ft^2
Bedroom 5

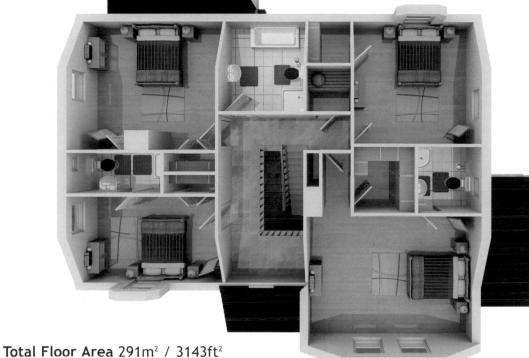

Total Floor Area 291m^2 / 3143ft^2

First Floor Plan

Rear Perspective View

Front Persepctive View

Dimensions

Kitchen	23.3m²	/ 252ft²
Dining	18.9m²	/ 204ft²
Living	40.7m²	/ 440ft²
Utility	11.1m²	/ 120ft²

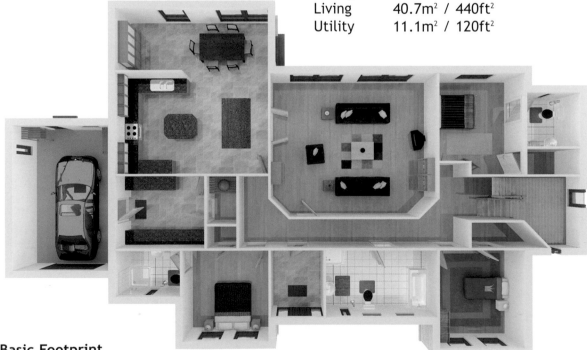

Basic Footprint

Width	19.8m²	/ 65ft²
Depth	12m²	/ 40ft²
Area	238m²	/ 2570ft²

Ground Floor Plan

Dimensions
Bedroom 1 14.5m² / 157ft²
Bedroom 2 13.3m² / 144ft²
Bedroom 3 14.4m² / 156ft²
Bedroom 4 20m² / 216ft²
Bedroom 5 27.4m² / 296ft²

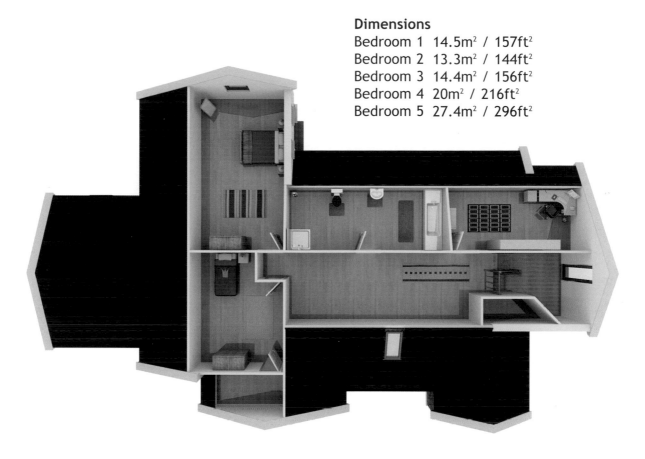

First Floor Plan   **Total Floor Area** 335m² / 3618ft²

Rear Perspective View

Front Persepctive View

Dimensions

Kitchen   15.6m² / 168ft²
Dining   15.6m² / 168ft²
Living   13.5m² / 146ft²
Utility   5.8m² / 63ft²

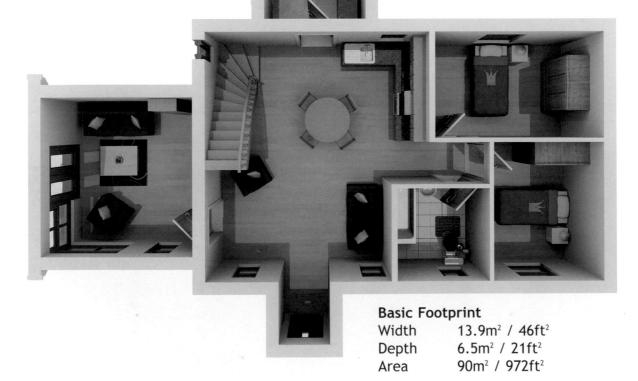

Basic Footprint

Width   13.9m² / 46ft²
Depth   6.5m² / 21ft²
Area   90m² / 972ft²

Ground Floor Plan

Dimensions
Bedroom 1 24.9m² / 269ft²
Bedroom 2 10m² / 108ft²
Bedroom 3 8.6m² / 93ft²

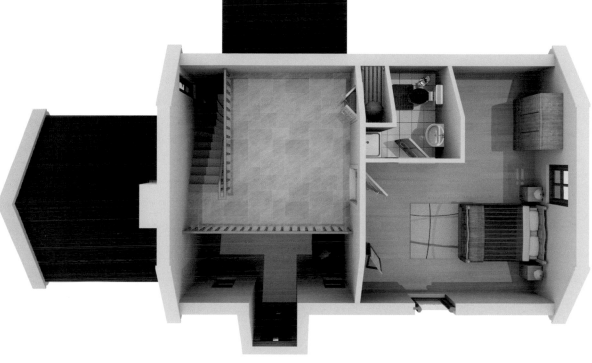

First Floor Plan

Total Floor Area 125m² / 1350ft²

Rear Perspective View

Front Persepctive View

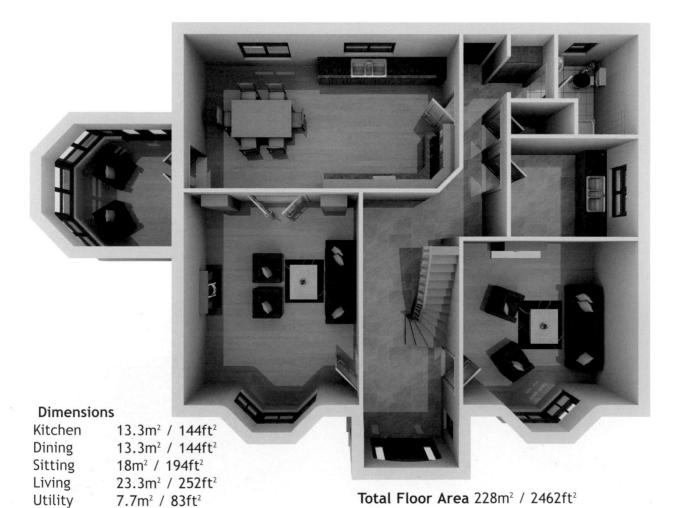

Dimensions

Kitchen	13.3m² / 144ft²
Dining	13.3m² / 144ft²
Sitting	18m² / 194ft²
Living	23.3m² / 252ft²
Utility	7.7m² / 83ft²

Total Floor Area 228m² / 2462ft²

Ground Floor Plan

Dimensions

Bedroom 1 16.7m² / 180ft²
Bedroom 2 18.5m² / 200ft²
Bedroom 3 13.5m² / 146ft²
Bedroom 4 12.8m² / 138ft²

Basic Footprint

Width   12m² / 40
Depth   9.9m⁷ / 33ft²
Area   119m² / 1285ft⁷

Rear Perspective View

Front Persepctive View

Dimensions

Kitchen	11.5m^2 / 124ft^2
Dining	15.5m^2 / 167ft^2
Living	54m^2 / 583ft^2
Utility	7.4m^2 / 80ft^2

Total Floor Area 230m^2 / 2484ft^2

Ground Floor Plan

Dimensions
Bedroom 1 22m^2 / 238ft^2
Bedroom 2 8.3m^2 / 90ft^2
Bedroom 3 13.8m^2 / 149ft^2
Bedroom 4 13.8m^2 / 149ft^2

Basic Footprint
Width   18.5m^2 / 61ft^2
Depth   9.5m^2 / 31ft^2
Area   176m^2 / 1896ft^2

First Floor Plan

Rear Perspective View

4. Landscape Design

Introduction

This section has been approached from a macro level, as it is not feasible to get into detail regards plant types, seasonal arrangements and levels of maintenance. However under recommended reading at the back of this book, there is a list of books and websites worth referencing.

The intention in this section is to advise on what can and should be done while you are in the process of visualising, designing and building your home.

Giving good consideration to what can and should be done with your site will have an impact on several areas:

- Privacy - whether indoors or out. You may have a lot of passing traffic and pedestrians, which you may not want to be seen by.
- Views - there may be a view you want to avoid obstructing or to frame with hedges, trees etc. On the other hand there may be an unsightly view or structure that needs to be hidden from certain viewing positions.
- Shelter - trees and hedges can drastically reduce wind exposure, which in turn reduces heat loss, making it easier and less costly to keep your home warm.

Trees block out traffic noise and wind

- Integration - by keeping existing hedgerows and trees or by adding hedges and trees, sculpted earth or fencing, or a combination of all you can lessen the visual impact of your house on the surrounding countryside.

Have a plan of what you want done to the site before any building work begins. It is best to have

any heavy machine work such as landscaping, removal of unwanted trees and rocks, or the installation of large boulders and other features done before building begins as it may not be safe or convenient to do so later.

Requirements

Gardening is an immensely broad topic. There are an endless number of garden types all with varying levels of maintenance requirements, there are very specific styles of garden and random mixes of all sorts. It can be overwhelming. The choice of garden you want, with how much time, effort and money you wish to put into it is a personal choice. A beautiful garden can be put together by a gardening contractor or by your-self over weekends, but it takes a continuous effort to keep it that way. Garden maintenance is a factor often overlooked, although there are garden layouts titled as low maintenance, nature will always insist on growing whon and where it can.

Finally, your chosen site and its location will have a bearing on what your options are. An exposed coastal site gets a different treatment throughout the year than a site that is inland and sheltered. Have a look around the area or similar areas and ask about the weather and its effect on growth and what can be grown.

Where to start?

Forward planning is always the best route to successfully attain what you want, especially since you are most probably building your house on a fresh green site, giving you a blank canvas for ground works and landscaping.

An existing tree as a focal point to be designed around

Take stock of what already exists on your site, it is important to take note of everything such as hedges, shrubs, trees embankments, the lie of the land, etc. as you may wish to integrate these natural features into your plans.

To help you decide on the type of garden you would like, look for ideas in other gardens, garden shows, the grounds of historic houses, books, TV and the Internet. Make notes and take photos of what you like and write down where you saw, read or heard this information as you may want to revisit it again.

As you form ideas for your garden from your notes and pictures, start assessing the amount of effort that will be required to create and maintain these ideas and how much skill you will need to learn, will become more evident.

Children's play equipment can require a sizable area

At this early stage it is vital to ask yourself the question "do I want to be an avid gardener and do I have the time to be one"? Another factor that is commonly overlooked is garden usage, what for and by whom? You may want one thing but circumstances dictate another, kids and pets don't go with prized rose beds, but there is always partitioning.

If you are unsure of what you want from a garden, a recommended interim measure is to sow grass over all areas of exposed soil. Some of the benefits of doing this are:

Keeps the site looking tidy and prevents weeds taking over

Stops the ground turning to mud and makes the areas usable for kids to play, clothes to dry and so on

Fixes the soil, stopping movement on slopped sites and the rinsing away of top soil in heavy rain

Designing your Landscape

The design part of the process can be virtually a hands-off process if you go down the road of hiring a Garden Designer. For a fee, a Garden Designer will go through your requirements and come up with a design proposal, schedule and estimated cost. This gives you the choice of implementing the proposal yourself, hiring a Landscape gardener to do it or engage the Garden Designer to project manage a contractor to complete it.

Alternatively it is possible to purchase pre designed garden layouts that can be modified or adapted to suit your site. These designs can come as a plan like an architectural drawing or as large sheets which you lay out on the ground and plant the named plants where marked, a form of gardening by numbers.

- And then, there is the DIY approach. For this you will require an accurate scale drawing of your site, your architect should be able to provide you with one. Make sure to include existing features that you plan to keep and note any large items outside your boundary that need to be considered when planning your garden. Include the direction of the prevailing wind and compass point north. This plan will greatly assist you in designing and planning your landscape.

For greater detail on designing your landscape get a copy of Garden Planning by Robin Williams, see page 171 for more information.

Preparing the garden site

Work begins by clearing the garden area of any stones, bricks, cement, timber etc. The soil should be cleared to a depth of between 250 & 300mm (10-12") with all removed items disposed of in a responsible manner off site.

If there is a notable presence of noxious weeds it might be best to eradicate them first. Check if it is better to use a weed-killer or to dig them out. If you plan on digging them out check on what type of weed they are because some weed types prosper by having their roots broken up, leading to more weeds not less.

DIY PH Testing Kit

Prior to digging and turning, it is worth testing your soil for its PH level (acidity or Alkalinity). DIY testing kits are available at garden centres. A loam soil is generally considered to be the best type as it is suitable for the widest range of plants, check the needs of the plants on your list against your soil type as they may not all be suitable for the soil type.

While you are doing all this digging and turning of the soil you might consider mixing in as much organic matter as possible, such as fresh-bagged compost or used mushroom compost, manure etc. This will work wonders for flowerbeds and the vegetable patch.

Hard or Soft?

Starting with the hard features of a garden first is generally best; these are patios, decking, paths, shed & green house foundations. Alternatively start with an existing feature such as a mature tree, if it is to be a focal point of your garden and everything else is to be worked around it. Working around or from an existing or primary feature can be an easy way to design your landscape, as there is a starting point to commence working from.

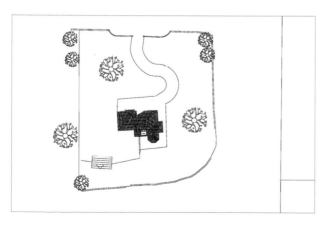

Scaled site plan

Once your hard features are positioned on a copy of your site drawing or traced overlay, it is time to start positioning your larger soft growing features such as bushes and trees etc. These need special attention as over the years they can get

Cherry blossom

very large, casting larger shadows, taking up a lot of space, blocking views and large roots can rupture foundations, walls, paths and patios.

As with everything you decide to plant in your garden, now or in the future, doing research beforehand will give great insight into the rewards your garden can bring. A list of recommended reading is at the back of this book. As mentioned earlier, do take a moment to consider how much time, effort and money you want to invest in your garden. If you are not sure, it is best to plan a low maintenance garden and see how you get on with it, as too much garden and not enough time will be disheartening and can lead to an unsightly wilderness.

With the design layout of your hard structural features and large growing features completed, it is time for flowers, shrubs, herbs and the like. These are generally contained or placed in flower beds, plant boxes, pots, urns, hanging baskets, etc. All but the flowerbeds are relatively mobile.

When marking out the plant positions and flowerbeds on your garden plan, keep in mind the areas of shadow and partial shade and the drainage needs of your plants. Check the plant's seasonal cycle to see at

what time of year it will flower, will it provide winter colour, etc? To find out more on plants and where best to plant them you would be best getting a book or two on the topic, see list on pg171.

Linking the house to the landscape

The house and landscaping of the garden need to

The dropped in look to well integrated

be designed together in order for them to integrate successfully into the surrounding

Front Persepctive View

Dimensions

Kitchen	24.5^2 / 265ft^2
Sitting	24.5^2 / 265ft^2
Utility	6.6^2 / 7.1ft^2

Basic Footprint

Width	16.2m^2 / 53.4ft^2
Depth	10.66m^2 / 35.2ft^2
Area	173m^2 / 1868ft^2

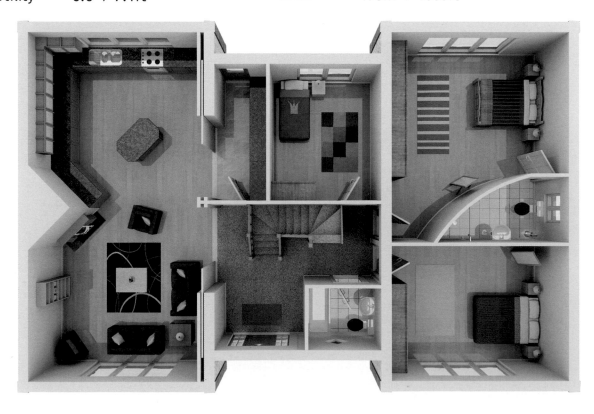

Ground Floor Plan

Dimensions
Bedroom 1 30.76m^2 / 332ft^2
Bedroom 2 20m^2 / 216ft^2
Bedroom 3 12.5m^2 / 135ft^2

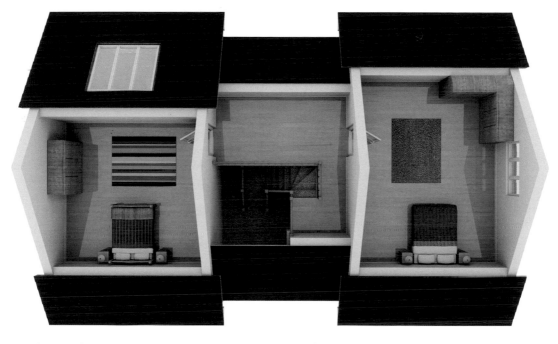

First Floor Plan   **Total Floor Area** 235m^2 / 2538ft^2

Rear Perspective View

Front Persepctive View

Dimensions

Kitchen	37.8m^2 / 408ft^2
Dining	21.2m^2 / 229ft^2
Sitting	36.9m^2 / 3994ft^2
Kitchen	26.4m^2 / 285ft^2
Living	14.76m^2 / 159ft^2
Sitting	15.13m^2 / 163ft^2
Dinning	15.13m^2 / 163ft^2

Basic Footprint

Width	24.1m^2 / 79.5ft^2
Depth	24.1m^2 / 79.5ft^2
Area	354m^2 / 3823ft^2

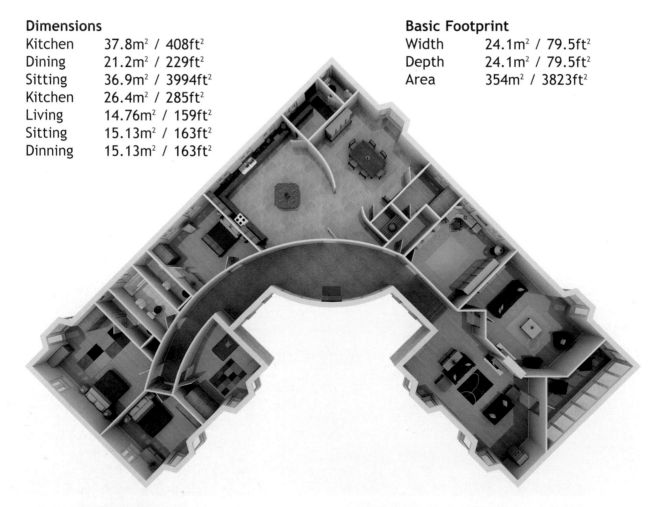

Ground Floor Plan

Total Floor Area 322m^2 / 3477ft^2

Home office

Rear Perspective View

Front Persepctive View

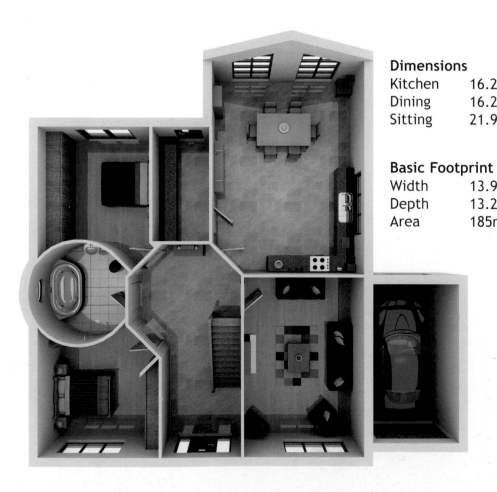

Dimensions

Kitchen	16.2m^2 / 175ft^2
Dining	16.2m^2 / 175ft^2
Sitting	21.9m^2 / 236ft^2

Basic Footprint

Width	13.9m^2 / 45ft^2
Depth	13.2m^2 / 43ft^2
Area	185m^2 / 1998ft^2

Ground Floor Plan

Total Floor Area 209m^2 / 2257ft^2

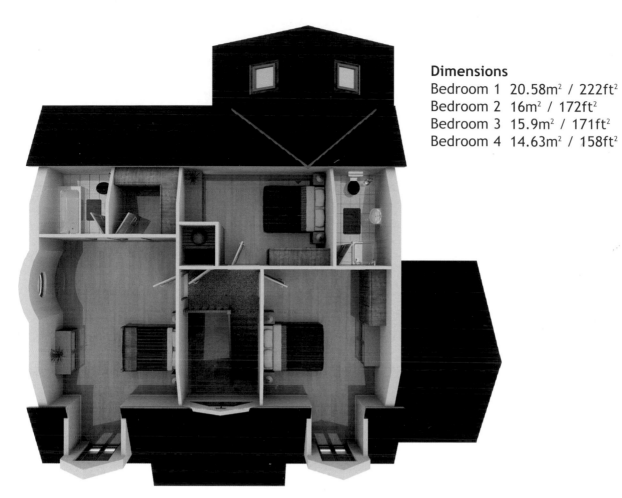

Dimensions
Bedroom 1 20.58m² / 222ft²
Bedroom 2 16m² / 172ft²
Bedroom 3 15.9m² / 171ft²
Bedroom 4 14.63m² / 158ft²

First Floor Plan

Rear Perspective View

Front Persepctive View

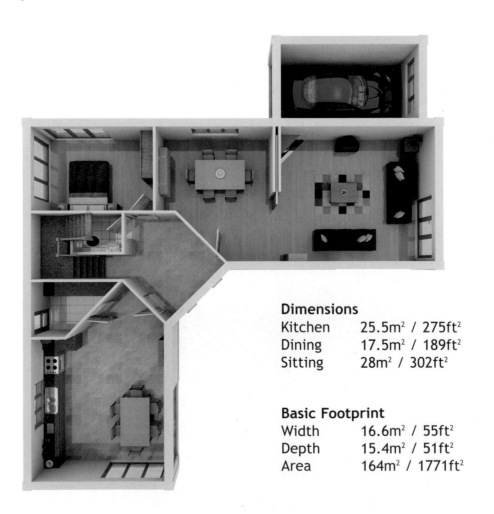

Dimensions
Kitchen   25.5m² / 275ft²
Dining   17.5m² / 189ft²
Sitting   28m² / 302ft²

Basic Footprint
Width   16.6m² / 55ft²
Depth   15.4m² / 51ft²
Area   164m² / 1771ft²

Ground Floor Plan

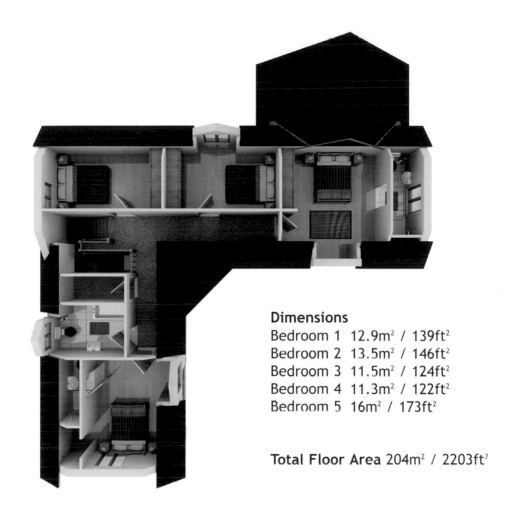

Dimensions
Bedroom 1 12.9m² / 139ft²
Bedroom 2 13.5m² / 146ft²
Bedroom 3 11.5m² / 124ft²
Bedroom 4 11.3m² / 122ft²
Bedroom 5 16m² / 173ft²

Total Floor Area 204m² / 2203ft²

First Floor Plan

Rear Perspective View

Front Persepctive View

Dimensions

Kitchen	19.7m² / 213ft²
Dining	18.3m² / 198ft²
Sitting	20.3m² / 219ft²

Basic Footprint

Width	17.5m² / 58 ft²
Depth	9m² / 30ft²
Area	158m² / 1701ft²

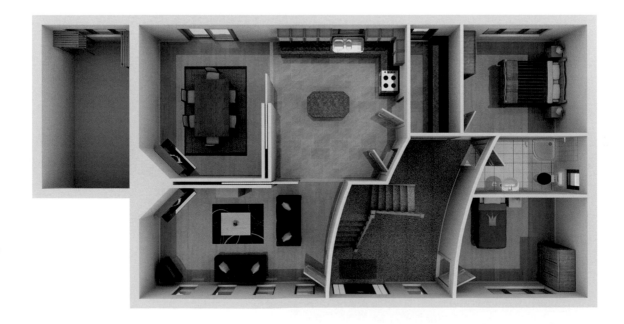

Ground Floor Plan

Dimensions
Bedroom 1 18m^2 / 194ft^2
Bedroom 2 12.8m^2 / 138ft^2
Bedroom 3 12.9m^2 / 139ft^2
Bedroom 4 27m^2 / 292ft^2

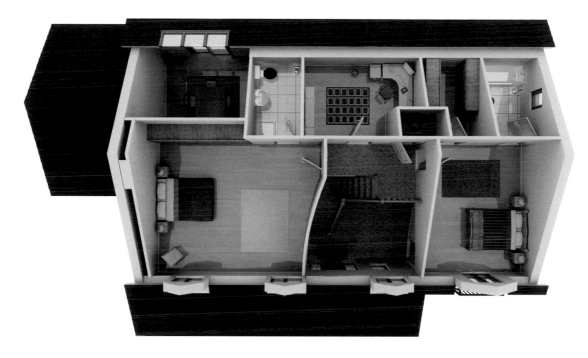

First Floor Plan

Total Floor Area 238m^2 / 2570ft^2

Rear Perspective View

Front Persepctive View

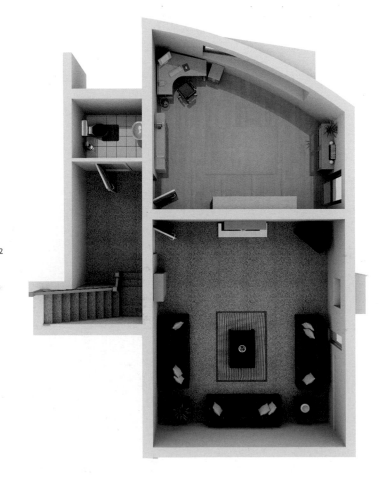

Dimensions

Kitchen	33.6m^2 / 363ft^2	
Dining	36.5m^2 / 394ft^2	
Sitting	38.7m^2 / 418ft^2	

Total Floor Area 336m^2 / 3629ft^2

Basic Footprint

Width	24.6m^2 / 81ft^2	
Depth	21.5m^2 / 71ft^2	
Area	529m^2 / 5713ft^2	

Ground Floor Plan

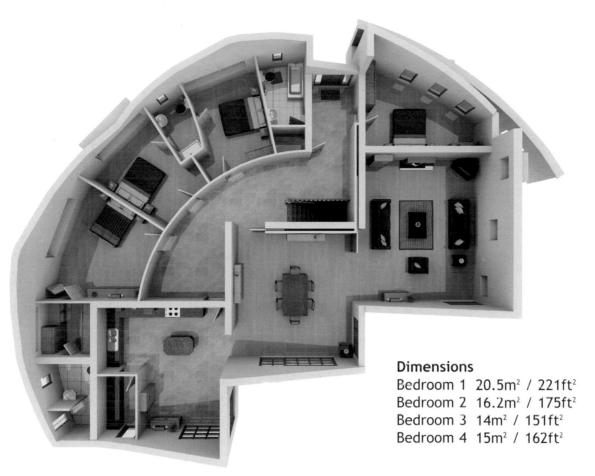

Dimensions
Bedroom 1 20.5m² / 221ft²
Bedroom 2 16.2m² / 175ft²
Bedroom 3 14m² / 151ft²
Bedroom 4 15m² / 162ft²

First Floor Plan

Rear Perspective View

Front Persepctive View

Basic Footprint
Width   12.7m^2 / 42ft^2
Depth   12.5m^2 / 41ft^2
Area   157m^2 / 1696ft^2

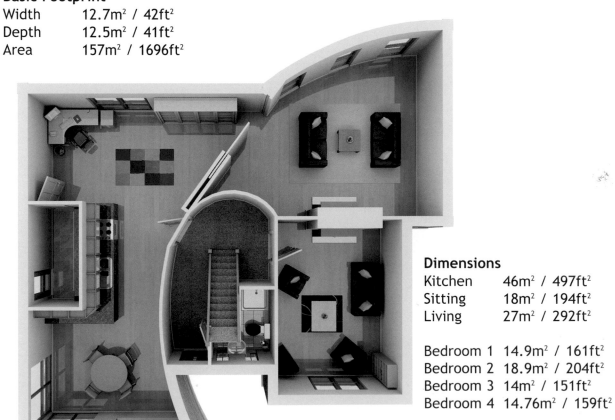

Dimensions
Kitchen   46m^2 / 497ft^2
Sitting   18m^2 / 194ft^2
Living   27m^2 / 292ft^2

Bedroom 1 14.9m^2 / 161ft^2
Bedroom 2 18.9m^2 / 204ft^2
Bedroom 3 14m^2 / 151ft^2
Bedroom 4 14.76m^2 / 159ft^2

Ground Floor Plan

Dimensions
Bedroom 1 14.7m^2 / 159ft^2
Bedroom 2 11.5m^2 / 124ft^2
Bedroom 3 14.3m^2 / 154ft^2
Bedroom 4 14.7m^2 / 159ft^2

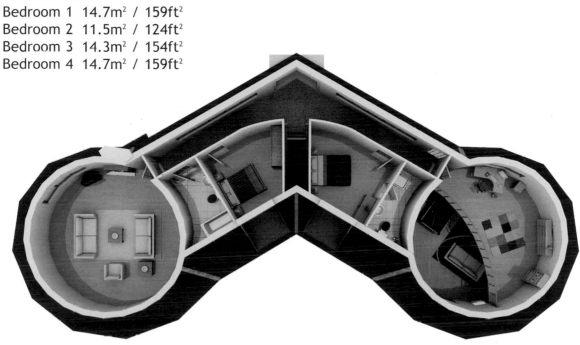

First Floor Plan

Total Floor Area 228m^2 / 2462ft^2

Rear Perspective View

Front Persepctive View

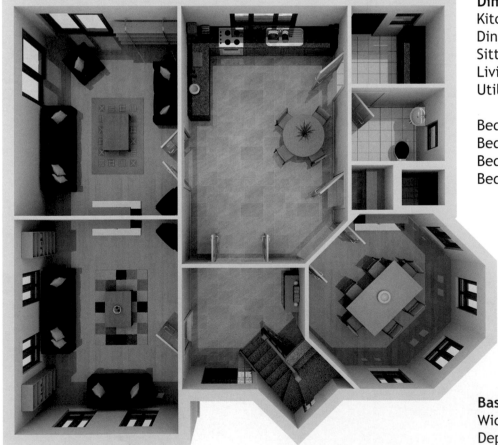

Dimensions

Kitchen	27.3m² / 295ft²
Dining	15.4m² / 166ft²
Sitting	23.1m² / 249ft²
Living	22.2m² / 240 ft²
Utility	20m² / 216ft²
Bedroom 1	14m² / 151ft²
Bedroom 2	18m² / 194ft²
Bedroom 3	18.7m² / 202ft²
Bedroom 4	17.5m² / 189ft²

Basic Footprint

Width	12.6m² / 42 ft²
Depth	11.5m² / 38 ft²
Area	145m² / 1566ft²

Ground Floor Plan

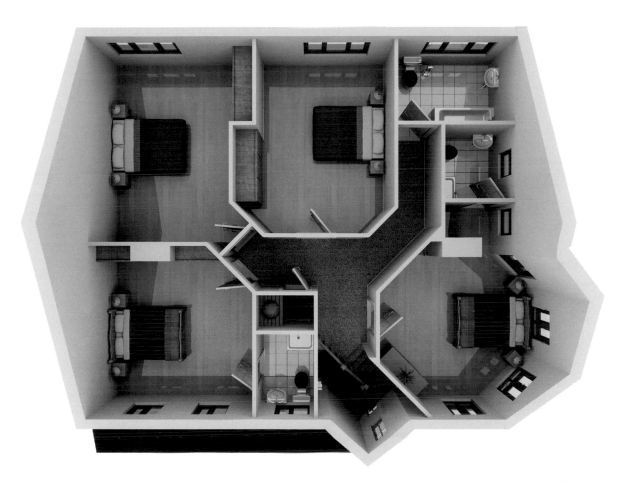

First Floor Plan

Total Floor Area 217m² / 2344 ft²

Rear Perspective View

Front Persepctive View

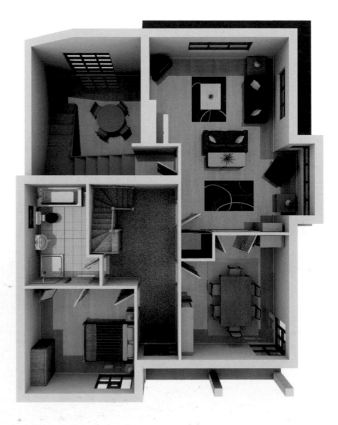

Ground Floor Plan

Dimensions

Kitchen	26.8m^2	289ft^2
Living	21.8m^2	235ft^2
Sitting	33.3m^2	360ft^2
Dining	16.7m^2	180ft^2
Bedroom 1	17m^2	184ft^2
Bedroom 2	12.2m^2	132ft^2
Bedroom 3	16m^2	173ft^2
Bedroom 4	14m^2	151ft^2

Total Floor Area 260m^2 / 2808ft^2

Basic Footprint

Width	9.8m^2	32ft^2
Depth	14m^2	46ft^2
Area	137m^2	1480ft^2

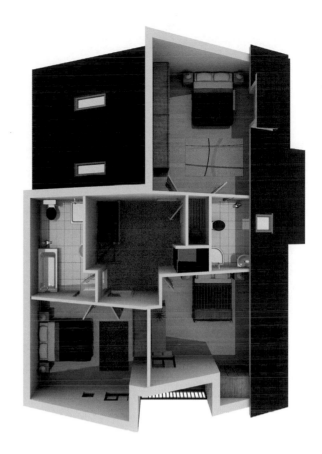

First Floor Plan

Rear Perspective View

Front Persepctive View

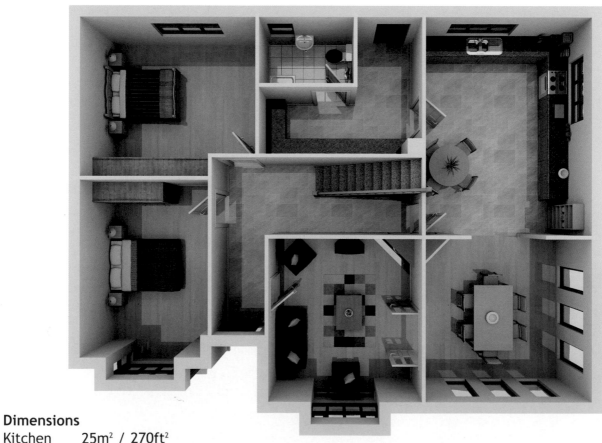

Dimensions

Kitchen   25m² / 270ft²
Sitting   17.4m² / 188ft²
Living   19.8m² / 214ft²

Total Floor Area 230m² / 2484ft²

Ground Floor Plan

First Floor Plan

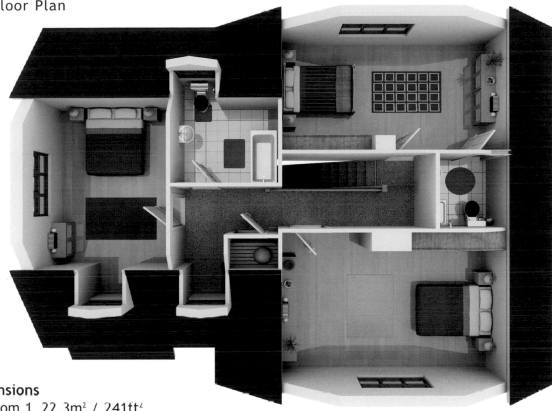

Dimensions
Bedroom 1 22.3m² / 241ft²
Bedroom 2 26.6m² / 287ft²
Bedroom 3 16m² / 173ft²
Bedroom 4 16m² / 173ft²
Bedroom 5 19.3m² / 208ft²

Basic Footprint
Width   14.1m² / 47ft²
Depth   10.8m² / 36ft²
Area   152m² / 1642ft²

Rear Perspective View

Front Persepctive View

Basic Footprint
Width   22.8m² / 75ft²
Depth   19m² / 63ft²
Area   433m² / 4676ft²

Dimensions
Kitchen   20.9m² / 226ft²
Dining   20.9m² / 226ft²
Sitting   30.7m² / 332ft²
Living   27.6m² / 298ft²

Bedroom 1 16.8m² / 181ft²
Bedroom 2 16.8m² / 181ft²
Bedroom 3 15m² / 162ft²
Bedroom 4 15m² / 162ft²

Total Floor Area 214m² / 2311ft²

Ground Floor Plan

Sitting Room

Rear Perspective View

Front Persepctive View

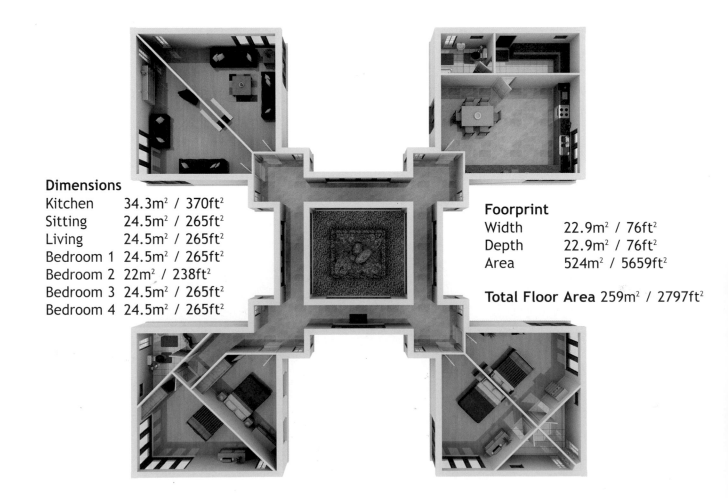

Dimensions

Kitchen	34.3m² / 370ft²
Sitting	24.5m² / 265ft²
Living	24.5m² / 265ft²
Bedroom 1	24.5m² / 265ft²
Bedroom 2	22m² / 238ft²
Bedroom 3	24.5m² / 265ft²
Bedroom 4	24.5m² / 265ft²

Foorprint

Width	22.9m² / 76ft²
Depth	22.9m² / 76ft²
Area	524m² / 5659ft²

Total Floor Area 259m² / 2797ft²

Ground Floor Plan

Kitchen with dining area

Rear Perspective View

Front Persepctive View

Dimensions

Kitchen	25.1m² / 271ft²
Sitting	14.37m² / 155ft²
Living	18.7m² / 202ft²

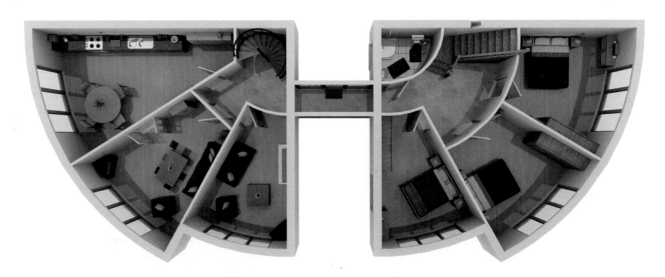

Basic Footprint

Width	26m² / 86ft²
Depth	15.7m² / 52ft²
Area	408m² / 4406ft²

Ground Floor Plan

Dimensions
Bedroom 1 28.3m^2 / 306ft^2
Bedroom 2 17m^2 / 184ft^2
Bedroom 3 17.3m^2 / 187ft^2
Bedroom 4 14.4m^2 / 155ft^2

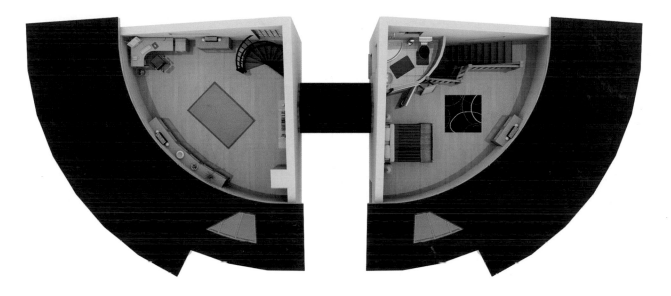

Total Floor Area 258m^2 / 2786ft^2

First Floor Plan

Rear Perspective View

Front Persepctive View

Dimensions

Kitchen	25.9m² / 280ft²
Dining	30.2m² / 326ft²
Sitting	36.4m² / 393ft²

Dimensions

Bedroom 1	30m² / 324ft²
Bedroom 2	13.1m² / 141ft²
Bedroom 3	9.6m² / 104ft²

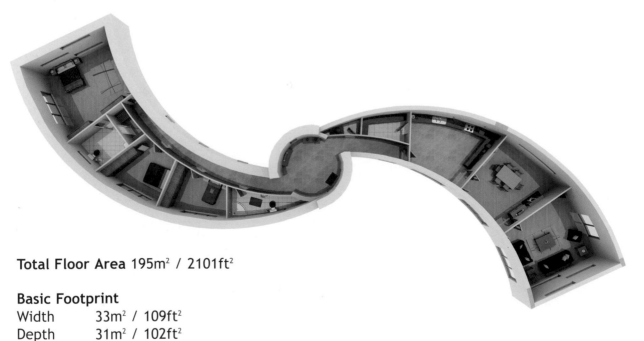

Total Floor Area 195m² / 2101ft²

Basic Footprint

Width	33m² / 109ft²
Depth	31m² / 102ft²
Area	1023m² / 11048ft²

Ground Floor Plan

Living Room

Rear Perspective View

Front Persepctive View

Dimensions

Kitchen	43m² / 464ft²
Dining	39.5m² / 427ft²
Sitting	32m² / 346ft²
Living	33.3m² / 360ft²

Total Floor Area 343m² / 3704ft²

Basic Footprint

Width	27.7m² / 91ft²
Depth	24m² / 79ft²
Area	665m² / 7182ft²

Dimensions

Bedroom 1	27.9m² / 301ft²
Bedroom 2	31.9m² / 345ft²
Bedroom 3	29.25m² / 316ft²
Bedroom 4	18m² / 194ft²

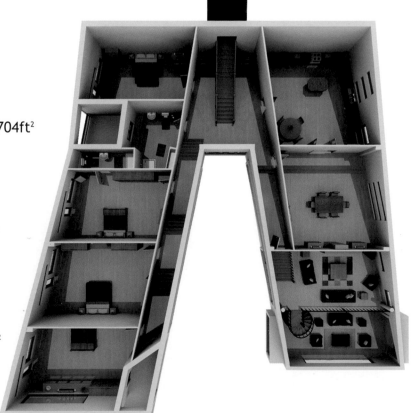

Ground Floor Plan

Dimensions
Bedroom 1 24.4m² / 264ft²
Bedroom 2 20.6m² / 222ft²
Bedroom 3 13.3m² / 144ft²
Bedroom 4 15.2m² / 164ft²

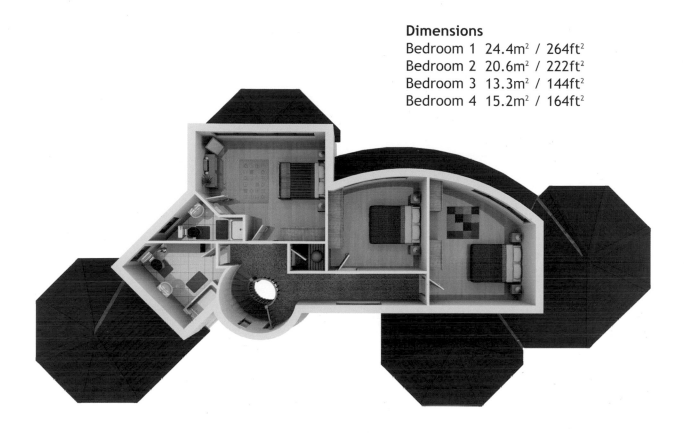

First Floor Plan

Rear Perspective View

Front Persepctive View

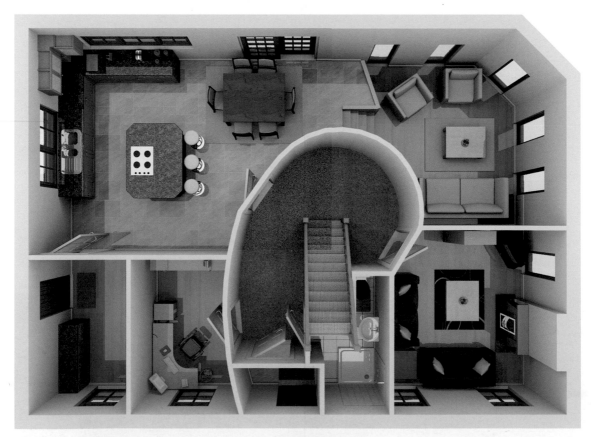

Basic Footprint

Width	12m² / 40ft²
Depth	8.8m² / 29ft²
Area	106m² / 1140ft²

Dimensions

Kitchen	28m² / 302ft²
Sitting	13.3m² / 144ft²
Living	12.3m² / 133ft²

Ground Floor Plan

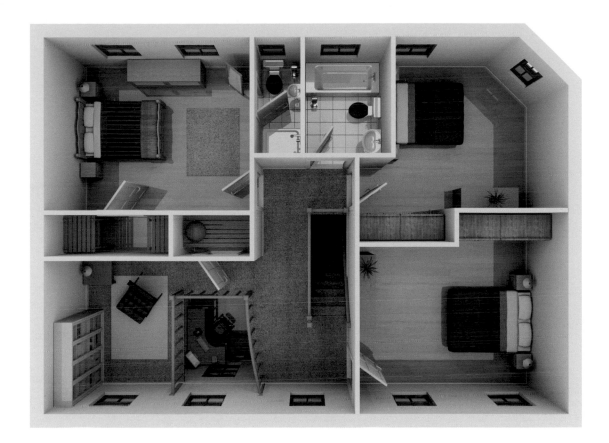

Total Floor Area 170m² / 1836ft²

First Floor Plan

Dimensions
Bedroom 1 21.3m² / 230²
Bedroom 2 16.4m² / 177ft²
Bedroom 3 14m² / 151ft²

Rear Perspective View

Front Persepctive View

Dimensions

Kitchen	30.6m² / 330ft²
Bedroom 1	11.9m² / 129ft²
Bedroom 2	9.8m² / 106ft²
Bedroom 3	6.8m² / 73ft²

Total Floor Area 78m² / 846ft²

Basic Footprint

Width	15.7m² / 52ft²
Depth	8.5m² / 28ft²
Area	134m² / 1442ft²

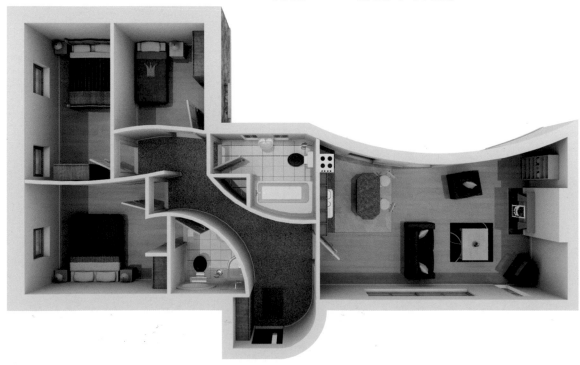

Ground Floor Plan

Sitting Room

Rear Perspective View

Front Persepctive View

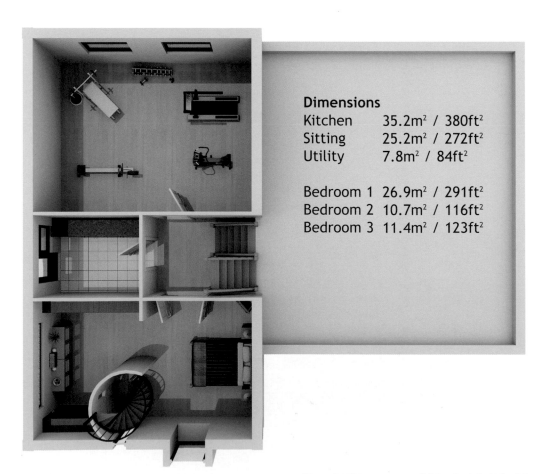

Dimensions
Kitchen   35.2m² / 380ft²
Sitting   25.2m² / 272ft²
Utility   7.8m² / 84ft²

Bedroom 1 26.9m² / 291ft²
Bedroom 2 10.7m² / 116ft²
Bedroom 3 11.4m² / 123ft²

Total Floor Area 229m² / 2469 ft²

Ground Floor Plan

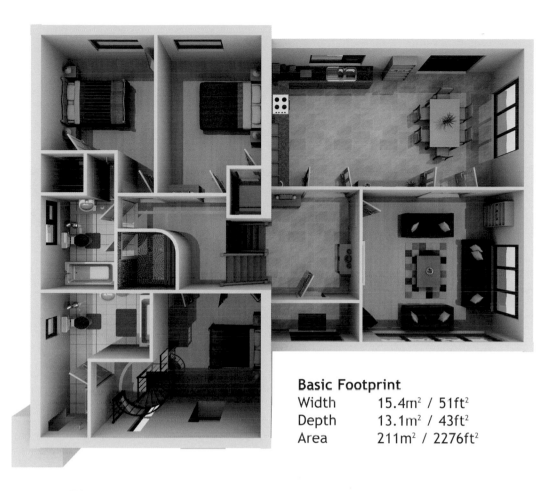

Basic Footprint

Width	15.4m² / 51ft²
Depth	13.1m² / 43ft²
Area	211m² / 2276ft²

First Floor Plan

Rear Perspective View

5. Environmental Impact & Energy Efficiency

Introduction

What do Environmental Impact and Energy Efficiency mean? They can be seen as the effects of the building and running of your house on the local and global environment. These areas can sometimes be overlooked, not because of their complexity but due to a lack of awareness or how they and others can actually benefit from them.

Your home exists in the global environment; it is a part of the ecological system that all things on the planet are part off. That may sound a little elaborate, and you might well ask what difference would my house make to the planet? Not much, but it will make a difference all the same. If for instance, you have a highly insulated house that uses 100 litres less of heating oil per year, this on its own will have minimal impact on the CO_2 released into the atmosphere, but, if 10,000 new homes were to save this much oil, that's a million litres of oil and that is a big difference.

It is estimated that 50% of the world's pollution comes directly and indirectly from homes. This includes the fuel we burn to heat, the chemicals we use to clean, the energy used to make the materials that your house is built of. For example the aggregate used in concrete has to be quarried, crushed, graded, transported to where the concrete is mixed, loaded into another truck and delivered to your site. All of this process requires diesel or electricity for the machines and vehicles, which is most probably generated through the burning of fossil fuels.

At all stages of the process there are opportunities to minimise the impact of your house on the environment through;
- The level of digging and foundation laying on your site to make it suitable for building upon
- The positioning of the house in relation to the sun and the elements of weather.
- The amount of concrete or timber required to build your design and where these products come from and how they are made (long distances, renewable forests, energy intensive processes).
- The level of insulation in your walls, windows and roof.
- The type of heating system and its layout

Environmental & Visual Impact

Any building, especially a home, is not a stand-alone entity in isolation from the rest of its physical and ecological surroundings. Its presence on the landscape gives it a visual impact. How well does it blend in or add to the landscape? When considering the visual impact of your home, keep in mind how it will add to the landscape. If travelling in an area for the first time and enjoying the beauty of the landscape, consider the existing houses and how they integrate into the environment.

Well integrated with privacy from roadside

Most sites for new houses are on what was formerly farmland. The hedge rows around many of these sites are inhabited by a variety of wildlife and the removal or damaging of these hedge rows displaces and can kill off this local wildlife. This in turn will have its own ecological knock-on effect.

The biggest environmental impact comes from the materials used in a building and the processes used to manufacture the materials :

"In the UK it is estimated that the production of building materials is responsible for about one-tenth of energy consumption and CO2 emissions" (Roaf 2003).

Calculating the exact impact of the manufacture and delivery of materials used in construction of a house and the impact of the every day running of the house are not a practical exercise for the self builder. What is recommended is to look at material options and the implications of using them. How are the materials made, where and what are their future energy benefits or lack of? Comparing building materials and products in this way, along with their cost and ease of use, will allow you to choose the best for you and the environment e.g. buying Irish or European timber requires far less transport than buying North or South American timber.

Assessing a materials impact requires the consideration of several factors *(Roaf 2003);*

- The energy required to produce the material
- The CO2 emissions resulting from the materials manufacture
- The Impact on the local environment resulting from the extraction of the material (e.g. quarry pit, wood taken from the forest, oil spill from an oil well, etc.)
- The toxicity of the material
- The Transportation of the material during its manufacture and delivery to the site
- The Degree of pollution resulting from the material at the end of its useful life.

Factors affected by material choice and design decisions;

- location and detailing of an architectural element
- maintenance required and the materials necessary for that maintenance
- contribution that the material makes to reducing the building environmental impact (e.g. insulation reduces heating and burning of fuel)
- flexibility of a design to accommodate changing uses over time
- Lifetime of the material and its potential for

reuse if the building is demolished.

Construction and positioning
Solar benefits
Positioning of the house to face south or within 15 degrees of South will attain the most amounts of heat energy or passive solar energy from the sun. Not all sites are suitable for south facing positions, which is worth considering when selecting a site. You are looking to have the most frequently used rooms on the south facing side of the house, to maximise the warmth of the sun and natural light.

Absorbing the best sun of the day during winter months will greatly reduce your heating bills and CO2 emissions, but position alone is not the only way to improved energy efficiencies of a house.

There are three steps to consider, the first is getting the energy into the house, second absorbing this energy for gradual release when the sun has set and third is controlling it through the variations of our climate.

Before making any decisions on design and methods of using the suns energy, there are several other considerations *(Roaf 2003):*

- How strong the sun is at different times of the year?
- Where the sun will be at different times of the year in relation to the site?
- How much of the sun's heat a building will need or not need, at different times of the year for the comfort of the occupants?
- What energy storage capacity should the building have in relation to the available solar gain to meet those needs?
- What the additional requirements are needed

in the design for controlling the heat gain from direct solar radiation, convection or conduction. How can the requirements be met by envelope performance, building form and ventilation?

Shelter

Strong winds force cold air into a house through any air leaks there might be and at the same time cools the outside surface of the house, especially when the outside is wet, this causes heat to transfer from the inside to the outside.

House sheltered at rear and narrow end to left

When laying out the site consider:

- Reduce wind exposure by orientating the narrow end of the building into the prevailing wind.
- Maximise the sheltering effect by spacing groups of buildings at around 6 times their height apart.
- Planting shelter-belts of trees about as high as the building and at a distance from the building of between 1 and 3 times the building's height;
- Courtyard layouts, L-shaped plans and walled gardens all create shelter and pleasant external spaces.

www.sustainabilityworks.org.uk

Materials and Construction

Building materials and their impact

"Embodied energy" why is this in inverted commas?, this is the amount of energy a material or product uses in its production and requires to be kept in working order. This can include everything from the mining of the raw material to the transport by ship and truck to its various locations of manufacture and assembly, and finally to your site.

Calculating the embodied energy can get quite detailed for example the process of pressing chipboard will require a certain amount of delivered electricity, but that electricity may have had to be generated from burning coal or oil. This level of calculation would be too much detail for most home builders. However by just asking a few questions, choosing materials and products on environmental grounds rather than price or convenience, can have a big impact. If we all do our bit, these bits add up, which does make a difference.

Further information can be attained through the references and links on pages 11-11

Insulation, Ventilation and areas of Heat Loss

Many houses when built have air leaks, thermal bridges and insufficient insulation through out. So before looking at environmentally friendly and renewable energies it is important to first have an energy efficient house with heat losses minimised from the roof, walls, floors and windows, as well as any air leakages from vents, extractor outlets and so on.

Building a closed entrance porch and having a back door that accesses the main house via a utility room or conservatory creates an air-lock which prevents the warm air of the house escaping when the doors are opened by preventing a through draft. These air-lock areas also preheat the cooler fresh air before it enters the house. Using the utility room as a place to wash and dry clothes will stop the moisture released leading to condensation and the potential for mould.

Thermal bridges are parts of the house made of materials that conduct heat and connect the interior to the exterior, such as concrete or steel lintels, steel ties, window frames or any solid masonry bridging the inside walls to the outside walls. The warmth within the house passes to the cooler outside by these bridges. The conductivity of materials is explained as follows;

> *"Aluminium conducts heat 4x better than steel, 170x better than glass, 1200x better than timber and PVC, and 2000x better than air."* (Roaf 2003)

To solve some of the heat loss issues the following is recommended:
- Nylon wall ties
- Split lintels above windows and doors where structurally suitable
- Use timber frame or aluminium windows with thermal spaces or seals e.g. the aluminium does not run continuous from the inside to the outside of the frame.
  Windows should be double or triple glazed
- with a high insulation value (suppliers will have details)
- Use a timber sub frame instead of returning brick work around walls and doors

Effective insulation and minimal areas of heat loss will reduce the energy required to heat your home and maximise on heat retention keeping it warmer for longer.

Let us look closer at ventilation. The control and quantity of ventilation will have an impact on your health and comfort in both winter and summer. Ventilation effects heating and cooling costs and assists in the prevention of mould in areas of condensation. There are various ways to ventilate a home, some are mandatory and must comply with building.

The following options are viable from a regulatory, cost and environmental perspective:

Windows that open:
These are an obvious standard to any home, but what can be overlooked is how windows open, how big the opening sections are and how is security effected while they are open. The ability to open a small window within a frame can allow for an amount of ventilation through out a winters day and with adequate locks, can be left open while you are out. Alternatively, in summer you will require the opening of as much window as possible in a frame to keep the house cool and fresh through out the day.

Passive Stack Ventilation:
This system depends on the warm stale air rising. An exit pipe is required in areas generating the highest quantities of stale air, such as the kitchen and bathroom. They will generate a continuous background airflow by sucking fresh air in from

other rooms. These air inlets and outlets can have humidity controls to increase or decrease airflow depending on the levels of moisture. Such passive systems have the advantage of very few moving parts, minimal maintenance and energy consumption

Trickle Vents:

This kind of vent is usually seen as slots in window frames and is generally required by building regulations unless a whole house ventilation system is being installed. If using just trickle vents, extractor fans will need to be installed in areas of high moisture creation such as the kitchen, bathrooms and utility room. Fitting the fans with humidity sensors will reduced their energy consumption.

Mechanical Ventilation & Heat Recovery (MVHR)
Such systems work best with well insulated houses were only the incoming fresh air requires heating. The system passes the outgoing stale air over a heat exchanger, which then provides the heat for the incoming fresh air. A good system can create the majority of the heating required for incoming air with the rest coming from a small heating element within the system. This type of system will only assist in the overall heating of a house. The fan fitted needs to use as little energy as possible if its cost is to be covered by the energy savings.

Heating, Ventilation & Air Conditioning (HVAC) systems are more commonly found in modern office buildings, but growing in home use. Although effective at regulating the temperature, humidity and quality of air within a building, they also come with several disadvantages. Firstly if not properly set-up or maintained they can incur a build up of bacteria which it then spreads

through the building. Secondly, it requires electricity, especially in summer for cooling, which in turn can cause CO_2 in its generating.

Light and Noise

Light
Bringing efficient natural light into most rooms is relatively simple due to the size of the average room and providing each room has at least one window. Quantity, quality and distribution contribute to the level of comfort and functionality that this natural light provides.

It is estimated that a window area equal to 10% of a rooms floor area will give a daylight factor of 1, which should be the absolute minimum, for an average room a window area of 15% will give a daylight factor of 2 and 25% area a factor of 3. (See following page for a visual reference)

What is "Daylight factor"? This is the amount of daylight falling on a horizontal surface of a room as a percentage of the daylight falling on a horizontal surface outside

(www.sustainabilityworks.gov.uk - 2005).

Long narrow rooms with one window in an end wall will suffer from glare near the window and dim light at the farther points. The best light to a room can be attained by having windows on two sides, this maximises the amount of direct light coming into the room during different times of the day. Better again for the amount of direct light per area is to install sky or roof lights. Twice as much light per area can be admitted into a room due to the ability of direct light to enter the room for more hours of the day. The effectiveness of direct light within a room is greatly affected by the interior

*Room = 48m² - Windows = 2.4m² (5%)

*Room = 48m² - Windows = 4.8*m² (10%)

*Room = 48m² - Windows = 7.2m² (15%)

*Room = 48m² - Windows = 12m² (25%)

visuals are impressions of the effects of window sizes

walls and furnishing colours as this will help reflect and balance the light within a room.

For areas that do not receive adequate light during daylight hours, the light they do get should be supplemented with lighting that compliments the natural light and does not create areas of heavy contrast or glare, which can lead to discomfort, eye strain and headaches. From an environmental perspective the use of long life eco bulbs should be used where possible as these use less energy and last longer.

Noise

External environmental noise would not be considered to be of general concern to the self-builder as your home is detached and on its own land. Depending where you choose to buy this land, there may be unwanted sounds from road, rail or air traffic and perhaps even nature.

The main areas to prevent disturbing noises is within the home, the most notable being uncarpeted staircases, hollow dry lined walls, wooden floors with no sound absorption between the boards and joists. Other noises can become apparent over time. For light sleepers, the sound from a car pulling into the drive may be disturbing, as would the sound from people chatting or watching TV. The positioning of rooms can also have an effect on the occupant's enjoyment as sounds from one room can be heard in another.

The following list on minimising potential sources

of environmental noise details this further:

- Using heavy construction materials
- Isolating elements of construction to break potential sound pathways
- Making sure there are no cracks or other air paths for sound to pass through
- Ensuring high standards of construction and detailing
- creating external barriers to muffle traffic noise
- Specifying high-quality windows with controlled ventilation
- Using sound-absorbing materials in cavity walls
- keeping drainpipe ducting away from living rooms and bedrooms

(www.sustainabilityworks.gov.uk - 2005)

Water Conservation

Although not the first thought that comes to mind when planning a house in Ireland, there are benefits to you and the environment. It is estimated that 65% of water usage is domestic. It is also estimated that with a few features and tweaks the average household, new or existing can reduce their usage by up to 50%.

Why do it?

For the environment. There are times during the year when water shortages do occur. The shortage may be due to reduced pressure caused by cracked pipes after heavy frost or reduced usage during time of drought. There is also the matter that whatever water your home uses has to be collected in a reservoir, treated and pumped to your house. In some cases you may have your own water source or a share in a well, the process requires energy and this energy can require the burning of fuel, which in turn leads

to CO_2 emissions. All this from using water! The difference one household makes by using water more conservatively may not be huge, but if ten thousand homes did it, there would be a very significant difference.

Other benefits of reduced water usage can be found in the type of showers you install, this would be apparent in your electricity or gas bills, there is also the benefit of the hot water lasting so everyone gets a good shower in the morning. Also many appliances like washing machines and dishwashers come with efficiency ratings using less water and power benefiting the environment and reducing running costs.

So before choosing your white goods, bathroom fittings and water sources do a little research into how you can make a difference, there are links and references at the back of this book to get you started.

Sewage Treatment

You will create sewage waste, whether from the toilet, shower, dishwasher or other. How ever it originates, it's got to be dealt with. The best solution, if available, is to connect directly to a mains sewage system. If this option is not available you can take the primary stage through a septic tank, where solids and up to half the organic matter are retained as solids and sludge, this will build up over time and require emptying every 1 - 4 years depending on the tanks size and your wastage.

Secondary treatment is the stage where effluent is released through a percolation area, reed bed or other. The effluent is spread out through these areas where it is absorbed by the earth or reeds.

Domestic Waste

How you dispose of your waste is worth investigating as landfills run out and those still active or closed, leak poisonous effluents into ground water and release greenhouse gases into the atmosphere. Not to mention bin collection charges, how you deal with your waste will have significant environmental and financial impacts.

Deciding how you are going to deal with your waste before designing your home will give you specific areas to deal with different types of waste and the appropriate means to disposing of it.

Separating and recycling

The first step is to separate your waste into organic, glass, metal, plastics, non recyclables and any other category suitable. As some of these categories build up and/or smell faster than others, you will need areas to store them until there is enough to deal with them in bulk. For example, bringing glass to a recycling bank may only be required once a month as with paper but organic and non recyclable waste may require dealing with every few days as the waste begins to decompose.

A compost heap is ideal for disposing of all your

Composting unit

organic and garden waste, with this combination making up to 50% of the average household's total waste, it will cut down plenty on bin collections and weight charges. Most domestic compost heaps will need approximately 2 - 3m sq of space and with most on off? homes being built on a quarter of an acre upwards. This should not be a problem and will provide you with good compost for your garden. For further information on composting talk to your local garden centre and look at garden/home shows.

Integrating your recycling into the house design will benefit the property's aesthetics and your day to day convenience. Many homes built ten years ago and older do not have adequate space for the variety of wheelie bins required. Nor do they have areas to store separated waste until collection or recycling day. This gives rise to bins being left around the side of the house and piles of recyclables in the shed or utility room. A great facilitator to recycling is convenience, if it is simplified, it is easy to get done, so if there are enough bins, bags, boxes close to hand there is no excuse not to separate the waste.

Renewable energy sources

Introduction

With the recognised change in climate conditions or global warming from the burning of fossil fuels it is imperative we all do what we can to reduce our dependency on such fuels by reducing our general energy usage. An estimated 25% of energy used in Ireland is home related, so if we all consume less and try to use energy from better sources, there would be a significant benefit to each household and to the wider global environment.

This year Ireland is being fined for not meeting its Kyoto Protocol undertaking, the country's CO2 emissions are too high. Many individuals believe this is entirely the responsibility of government and big business but as stated already, 25% of energy consumed in Ireland is in our homes, making it all our responsibility.

On an individual household level, the benefits of a well insulated building, fitted with energy efficient appliances and heating systems are; reduced fuel bills and a better standard of living, as your home will be easier to heat, keep warm and all at a reduced cost.

Another factor that should be considered is the limited supply of fossil fuels. Although there are no exact figures to the quantities of coal, oil and gas reserves left on the planet. Petroleum Intelligence weekly estimated that in 2003 the top 20 oil companies and governments had total oil reserves of about 900billion barrels, that may seem a lot, but with the world using 82million barrels a day and this figure growing, these reserves will last 30years or less.

82m Barrels of oil are used globally per day

Designing your home to be less dependent on oil products is a smart move for future proofing your home and to help reduce our carbon emissions. Many people will quite happily work long hours and dedicate weekends to insuring their children have the best childhood experiences and opportunities in life so, how environmentally friendly and energy efficient your home is will have a direct impact on you and your family in the decades to come.

Initial steps

Before looking at renewable energy sources it is worth mentioning the initial steps, these are discussed in the section on House design pg13.

Insulation

A well insulated house requires less energy to heat and when heated stays that way for longer, cuts bills and gives greater thermal comfort to the inhabitants. This area is discussed in greater detail earlier.

Solar Energy

Passive Solar Heating

This is simply heating areas direct from the sun. It starts by facing the house directly south or within 15° and having 50% of the vertical surface high quality double or triple glazed, this allows the sunlight in and little heat out. The sunlight is best falling on a concrete wall, and or the floor (Slate or dark coloured tiles) to enable the sunlight to become heat energy, these surfaces slowly heat up during the day and just like a storage heater, gradually releasing this heat after the energy supply has stopped. Sun rooms and conservatories are designed to maximise the suns energy, warming quickly. To maximise these benefits it is important to close curtains after the sun has set to keep as much heat in as possible.

Water Heating

There are various cost effective and efficient ways to heating water from the suns visible and infrared rays.

- Flat radiator format - these are relatively easy to install on an exterior surface but are unable to absorb a high percentage of the energy falling on them and in cold temperatures may loose more energy than gaining.

Water heating Panels - *www.nrel.gov*

- Thermal vacuum tubes - as the tubing is well insulated by a vacuum like tea in a thermos flask, this type of system is very efficient. Very easy for the contents to gain heat but very hard to loose it.

- Computerised tracking collectors - either of the listed options can be fitted to a tracking system that simply rotates the panel so it is facing the sun at the optimum angle and tilt at all times, but may remove any cost savings over the life span of the system due to its instillation costs.

With all these systems water is passed through the collector and fed into a hot water tank and can be heated further by an emersion or boiler system if required.

calculator, except on a far larger and more efficient scale. There are a variety of panel types producing differing levels of power per square metre, with cost reflective in this. PV panels covering an area of 10sq M an average home could generate up to 30% of its own power. 100% sustainability would require a costly amount of panels and the problem of storing the power for use during the hours of darkness is not realistically feasible at

photovoltaic (PV) panels
www.nrel.gov

present. Power is stored in battery banks contained in a garage or basement for use at night or during periods of high electrical usage.

photovoltaic (PV) panels - *www.nrel.gov*

As you are in the process of planning your home, it may be worth considering increasing this area by using the PV panels as a replacement material for the roof, this will reduce the cost of paying for both tiles and PV panels.

Solar Power

This is a simple process of converting the suns light energy into electrical energy through photovoltaic (PV) panels, very similar to a solar

Wind Power

For average wind speed in Ireland is second only to Scotland, making it an ideal

Domestic wind turbine
www.nrel.gov

location for harnessing this great power source. With an ability to create up to 2.5KW, domestic wind turbines can contribute significantly to your renewable energy. As a guide to usage 1KW = 1000watts, most light bulbs use 60watts/hr, microwaves 700watts/hr. As with generating electricity from solar panels, this source of power will not supply 100% of your power needs but could make a significant contribution.

Biomass energy

What is it? It is the use of any naturally occurring material ie wood, plant matter, cow slurry, most waste material that is available on a renewable basis. These materials are burnt, contained for gasification or fired with fossil fuels. Images The

Biomass fuel in the form of wood chips

most common for domestic use is wood which when growing* absorbs as much CO_2 as when burnt, making it an ideal renewable energy source. For burning in modern stoves it comes in the form of pellets. These stoves are sealed units with some having glass fronts for better

Growing trees for Biomass fuel
www.nrel.gov

aesthetics, with efficiency levels between 75 & 90% which is considerably better than a traditional open fire with an efficiency level of just 20% with its remaining heat energy going up the chimney.

* Once a tree reaches maturity and its growth slows it absorbs less CO_2 and adversely gives out less oxygen.

Grants & Initiatives

In some European countries there are grants for installing renewable energy systems, although at the time of writing we are unaware of any in the Republic of Ireland, but do check with your architect, county council and government websites. For the North there is assistance, check out www.clear-skies.org for available grants and assistance. Research Grants. There are links to websites on page 172 where you can get informed and keep up to date.

6. References & Links

County Council Planning Offices

Carlow County Council
County Offices
Athy Rd
Carlow
(059) 9170306
ogleeson@carlowcoco.ie
www.carlow.ie

Cavan County Council
Courthouse
Cavan
Co. Cavan
049 4331799
www.cavancoco.ie

Clare County Council
1 Westgate Business Park,
Kilrush Road, Ennis.
Co. Clare
(065) 6846232
planoff@clarecoco.ie
www.clarecoco.clare.ie

Cork County Council
County Hall
Cork City
Co. Cork
(021) 4276891
www.corkcoco.ie

Donegal Co Council
Creeslough Dunfanaghy
Drumfin
Co. Donegal
(074) 35356
www.donegalcoco.ie

Dun Laoghaire Rathdown County
Council
County Hall
Marine rd
Dun Laoghaire
(01) 2054700
planning@dlrcoco.ie
www.dlrcoco.ie

Fingal County Council
County Hall,
Swords,
Co. Dublin
(01) 8905000
info@fingalcoco.ie
www.fingalcoco.ie

Galway County Council
Aras an Chontae,
Prospect Hill,
Galway.
(091) 509308
planning@galwaycoco.ie
www.galwaycoco.ie

Kerry County Council
Rathass,
Tralee,
Co. Kerry
066 7183500
kcc@kerrycoco.ie
www.kerrycoco.ie

Kildare County Council
St Mary's
Naas
Co. Kildare
(045) 873829
www.kildare.ie/countycouncil/

Kilkenny County Council
County Hall
John st
Kilkenny
056 - 7794010
planning@kilkennycoco.ie

Laois County Council
Aras an Chontae
Portlaoise
Co. Laois
0502 64000
internet@laoiscoco.ie
www.laois.ie

Leitrim County Council
Carrick-on-Shannon
Co. Leitrim
071 9650450
ctracey@leitrimcoco.ie
www.leitrimcoco.ie

Limerick County Council
County bldgs
Dooradoyle,
Limerick
061 - 496000
secretar@limerickcoco.ie
www.limerickcoco.ie

Longford County Council
Great Water St.
Longford.
043-43427
planning@longfordcoco.ie
www.longfordcoco.ie

Louth County Council
County Hall,
Millennium Centre, Dundalk.
Co. Louth
(042) 9353180
planning@louthcoco.ie
www.louthcoco.ie

Mayo County Council
Aras an Chontae
Castlebar
Co. Mayo
(094)902 44 44
Planning@mayococo.ie
www.mayococo.ie

Meath County Council
County Hall
Navan
Co. Meath
(046)9077238
planning@meathcoco.ie
www.meathcoco.ie

Monaghan County Council
County Offices
The Glen
Monaghan
047 30500
secretar@monaghancoco.ie
www.monaghan.ie

Offaly County Council
Aras an Chontae,
Charleville Road, Tullamore
Co. Offaly
0506 46800
planning@offalycoco.ie
www.offaly.ie

Roscommon County Council
The Courthouse
Roscommon Town
Co. Roscommon
090 6637184
pcassidy@roscommoncoco.ie
www.roscommoncoco.ie

Sligo County Council
County Hall,
Riverside, Sligo,
Co Sligo
071 9156666
info@sligococo.ie
www.sligococo.ie

Tipperary North Co Council
Civic Offices,
Limerick Road, Nenagh
Co. Tipperary
(067) 31771
planning@northtippcoco.ie
www.northtippcoco.ie

Tipperary South County Council
Aras An Chontae
Clonmel
Co. Tipperary
052 34455
planning@southtippcoco.ie
www.southtippcoco.ie

Waterford County Council
Civic Offices,
Dungarvan,
Co. Waterford
058 22057
planninginfo@waterfordcoco.ie
www.waterfordcoco.ie

Westmeath County Council
County Building,
Mount Street,
Mullingar
Co. Westmeath
044-32000
planning@westmeathcoco.ie
www.westmeathcoco.ie

Wexford County Council
County Hall
Wexford
Co. Wexford
(053) 76500
planning@wexfordcoco.ie
www.wexford.ie

Wicklow County Council
County Buildings
Wicklow
Co. Wicklow
(0404) 20100
plandev@wicklowcoco.ie
www.wicklow.ie

Antrim District Council
Council Offices,
The Steeple,
Antrim, BT41 1BJ
028 9446 3113
info@antrim.gov.uk
www.antrim.gov.uk

Armagh District Council
The Council Offices
The Palace Demesne
Armagh
BT60 4EL
(028) 3752 9600
info@armagh.gov.uk
www.armagh.gov.uk

Derry City Council
98 Strand Road,
Derry,
BT48 7NN
(028) 7136 5151
info@derrycity.gov.uk
www.derrycity.gov.uk

Down District Council
24 Strangford Rd,
Downpatrick,
BT30 6SR Co. Down
(028) 4461 0800
council@downdc.gov.uk
www.downdc.gov.uk

Fermanagh District Council
Townhall,
Enniskillen,
Co. Fermanagh, BT74 7BA
(028) 6632 5050
fdc@fermanagh.gov.uk
www.fermanagh.gov.uk

Tyrone District Council
The Grange,
Mountjoy Road, Omagh,
Co. Tyrone BT79 7BL
028 8224 5321
info@omagh.gov.uk
www.omagh.gov.uk

Books

Alan Titchmarsh
Complete book of gardening
BBC Worldwide Ltd
ISBN; 0 563 53401 X

Peter F. Smith
Eco-refurbishment - A guide to saving & producing energy in the home
Architectural Press
ISBN: 0-7506-5973-4

Robin Williams
Garden Planning
The Royal Horticultural Society
ISBN: 1 84000160 7

Victor Papanek
The Green Imperative
Thames & Hudson
ISBN: 0-500-27846-6

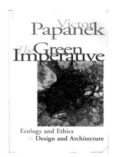

David Stevens, Lucy Huntington & Richard Key
The Complete book of Garden Design, Construction & Planting
Cassell Paperbacks
ISBN: 1-84188-172-4

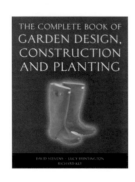

Irish Rural Dwellers Association
Positive Planning for Rural Houses
Irish Rural Dwellers Association
ISBN: 0-9547926-0-2

John Brookes
Garden Design Book
Dorling Kindersley Ltd
ISBN: 0-86318-638-6

Colin Buchanan & Partners, Mike Shanahan & Partners and Cork County Council
Cork Rural Design Guide
Cork County Council
ISBN: 0 9525 86940

Sue Roaf with Manuel Fuentes & Stephanie Thomas
Ecohouse 2 - A design guide
Architectural Press
ISBN: 0 7506 5734

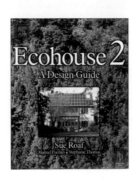

Homebond
Homeowner's handbook
National House Building Guarantee Company Ltd
ISBN: 0-9523614-9-3

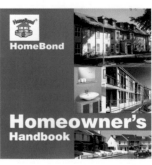

Websites

Environmental Impact & Energy Efficiency

www.irish-energy.ie

www.sustainabilityworks.gov.uk

www.clear-skies.org

www.greenphase.com/

www.wwflearning.co.uk/news/viewpoint_0000000713.asp

www.century.ie/cent/ecohouse.asp

www.channel4.com/4homes/ontv/grand-designs/houses/S/suffolk_eco_house.html

www.thearchitectureroom.com/SustainableHouses.html

www.thehouseplanner.co.uk/

www.biomass.org/

http://edugreen.teri.res.in/explore/renew/biomass.htm

www.solar4power.com/

http://home.earthlink.net/~fradella/green.htm

www.ecobusinesslinks.com

Finding a Site

www.landregistry.ie/

www.daft.ie/

www.myhome.ie/

www.sitefinderireland.com/

http://sites.propertyireland.net

Eugene Farrell, John A. McCarthy & Anthony McFeely
House Building Manual
National House Building Guarantee Company Ltd
ISBN: 0-9523-6144-2

Tony Booth & Mike Dyson
Build Your Own Home
How to Books
ISBN: 1-85703-901-7

Paul J Grimaldi
Getting the builders in
Elliot Right Way Books
ISBN: 0-7160-3012-8

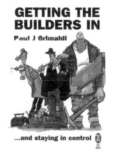